TIN HOUSE
MAGAZINE

A fashionable milieu is one in which everybody's opinion is made up of the opinions of all others. Does everybody have a different opinion? Then it is a literary milieu.

— *Marcel Proust*

VOLUME 1 • NUMBER 3

DAWN POWELL

as you've never seen her

Sunday, Monday, and Always, initially published in 1952, was Dawn Powell's own personal selection of her best short stories. In this new, expanded edition, four fresh stories have been added.

Sunday, Monday, and Always
Stories by Dawn Powell

Dawn Powell always dreamed of becoming a successful playwright, and wrote ten plays over forty years. This volume contains the only two plays to be mounted during her lifetime — *Big Night* and *Jig Saw* — as well as two yet unproduced gems, *Women at Four O'Clock* and *Walking Down Broadway*.

Four Plays by Dawn Powell
Edited and with an Introduction by
Michael Sexton and Tim Page

1-800-639-7140 • www.steerforth.com

Other titles by DAWN POWELL available from
STEERFORTH PRESS

The Diaries of Dawn Powell • *The Golden Spur* • *My Home is Far Away*
• *The Locusts Have No King* • *Come Back to Sorrento* • *The Wicked Pavilion* • *Angels on Toast* • *The Bride's House* • *A Time to be Born* •
The Happy Island • *Turn, Magic Wheel* • *Dance Night*

LETTERS

We welcome all of the mail that you have showered upon us. Jean Nathan's story 'The Secret Life of the Lonely Doll' appears to have been a virtual madeleine for scores of readers who were not only delighted to rediscover the strange and wonderful children's-book classic, 'The Lonely Doll,' but shocked to discover the surreal hidden life of author Dare Wright. Many echoed the sentiment of Mildred Baker of Wisconsin, who found the article "so-oo sad." Our favorite letter of the month, however, has to be the following:

Tin House Issue No. 2
Fall 1999

• WOLFE BITE •

Dear Walter:

Your article on your recently published novel *Thumbsucker* in the second issue of *Tin House* really disturbed me. Is it masochism or sarcasm? I was hoping the latter, but by the time I finished reading it seemed like you derived pleasure from shooting yourself in the foot.

It gave me the creeps to read you discussing your own work

as if you'd just woken from a bad dream and couldn't remember writing such an "offensive" thing. Where's your pride, buddy? Dissing yourself is a really lame way of excusing yourself for what you percieve to be the mistakes with your story. How 'bout chalking it up to the learning curve of your own development as a writer? Hindsight is supposed to be 20/20. To say such and such happens for reasons "one supposes," or to ask questions surely you know the answer to, makes me wonder, were you or were you not there when the novel was written?

Okay, so maybe you don't want to defend yourself against Mr. Wolfe's attack, but forcing us to view your self-analysis is like forcing someone to look at a bloody, gaping flesh wound with the bone exposed. It's gross and embarrassing.

What was the point in writing this article? Beating the critics to the punch? Is this a way of waiving responsibility in case they agree with Mr. Wolfe?

If you're worried about the decay of American literature, I'd say you exposed a few cavities with this kind of piece. What's wrong with writing *your* reflections of *your* era. You're writing what you know. (I'm assuming you're in your thirties or forties unless that picture with your bio is really old). Tom's from a different generation. While I applaud him for wanting to maintain standards, he can't halt progress. Writers are going to express themselves in the way their environment has shaped them. You're giving him far too much weight. It's his opinion for God's sake, not an edict. It seems you're allowing a man to erode your self-confidence based on him reading the title of your book!!!! If you admire the man, then praise him. Flogging yourself with his whip is a twisted way to express hero worship.

Writers aren't supposed to review themselves. There's a little thing called "objectivity," that unless you have multiple personalities is impossible to achieve in regards to your own work.

All I can say is your publisher must be so pissed at you right now. I'm picturing this book tour where you're sitting in Barnes & Noble telling people *not* to buy your book. While the pity angle might work, I don't think reverse psychology will.

You've made me so sad I feel like curling up in the corner and sucking my thumb.

Chin up, Walter. Silence is golden. Develop some mystery. In pointing out your own flaws you've defeated the whole purpose of getting people to read a new novel.

Sincerely,
Currie Alexander Powers

Editors' Note

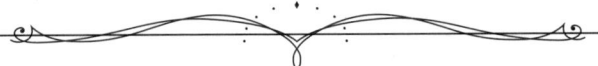

Thank you for picking up issue 3. And thank you (if it is you) for giving the first two issues such a warm welcome. *Tin House* is now available in over five hundred bookstores across the country and around the world.

Continuing our formula of having no formula, issue 3 features a previously unpublished interview with the satirist Dawn Powell, the brilliant chronicler of bohemian New York from the thirties through the sixties. After nearly falling off the literary map, Powell has roared back into print and prominence due in no small part to her biographer Tim Page, who provides the introduction to Robert Hethmon's interview, Powell's last, from August 1965. Although dying of stomach cancer, Powell diplomatically dishes on her disastrous collaboration with Stella Adler and the Group Theatre, the strident practitioners of Method acting.

There are also profiles of blacklisted writer John Sanford and Mian Mian, mainland China's underground literary sensation whose transgressive writing about sex, drugs, and rock 'n' roll has caused her to be dubbed the Poster Child for Spiritual Pollution. *Tin House 3* offers nothing millennial, but does contain profound meditations on mortality by poet Yehuda Amichai, a chilling story by Amy Hempel, and possibly the only thing that could unite Jane Austen, Alice B. Toklas and Erskine Caldwell—apple pie. The cover story, "The Devil is a Poet," is by one of this century's most fabulous poets and essayists, Charles Simic, who undertakes a pilgrimage into the heart of Hieronymus Bosch's *Temptation of Saint Anthony*, divining the comedy and horror inherent in art, poetry, and faith.

Enjoy.

FICTION

12 Amy Hempel · BEACH TOWN
"I didn't have to hide to listen."

26 Mian Mian · AN EXCERPT FROM *CANDY*
"I am every mother's nightmare."

73 John Sanford · AN EXCERPT FROM *A PALACE OF SILVER*
"But most painful, most piercing, was a sight of what she'd worn."

112 Lisa Zeidner · CHOSEN PEOPLE
"To commit a sexual act in the face of death was therefore not sacrilege but sanctimony."

132 J. Robert Lennon · MAILMAN
"Words like 'mail fraud' and 'mandatory sentencing' pass through his mind."

NEW VOICES

158 **Fiction:** James Conrad · ROAD
"A high-school English teacher only has so many chances in life to get out, and I took mine the moment it came."

180 **Poetry:** Chin Ho Chong · SMOKE

POETRY

36 Pattiann Rogers · Stone Bird

93 Yehuda Amichai · All the Motions and Positions
· Life is Called Life
· And What is My Life Span?

97 Nicholas Christopher · *from* 1972

154 Marge Piercy · Vanity, vanity

156 Ed Ochester · Chickadee

175 David Lehman · February 28
· April 4

177 Celia Gilbert · For the Bees

VOLUME ONE — NUMBER THREE — WINTER 2000

INTERVIEWS · PROFILES

14 CRUEL CITIES
Jonathan Napack profiles China's "Poster Child for Spiritual Pollution," the Chinese Gen-X cult sensation Mian Mian, author of "Candy" (excerpted on page 26), who is openly transgressive both in her personal life and on the page.

38 MEMORIES OF THE GROUP THEATRE
The final, never-before-published interview with Dawn Powell, one of the greatest comic novelists of the twentieth century, on her ill-fated collaboration with Stella Adler and the Group Theatre in 1932. Introduction by Tim Page, Powell's biographer and the man responsible for bringing Powell back into the public eye.

55 VISITING MR. SANFORD
Neil Gordon profiles John Sanford, the ninety-four-year-old contemporary of Nathanael West, a prolific realist and outspoken leftist known for his defiance of McCarthy's House Un-American Activites Committee.

PILGRIMAGES

102 Charles Simic · THE DEVIL IS A POET
The poet ventures to Lisbon's Museu de Arte Antiga to lose himself in the surreal universe of the sixteenth-century triptych "The Temptation of Saint Anthony."

122 Lynne Tillman · DESPERATELY SEEKING JANE AND PAUL BOWLES
Swirling sands, camels, vicious lovers, the Bowleses had it all going on. Tillman goes in search of father figure Paul Bowles.

LOST AND FOUND

81 Frank Bures on the lost brother, Shiva Naipul. V.S. Naipaul won the war of sibling rivalry on the battleground of fame and letters. But was his younger brother Shiva the better writer?

84 Gerald Howard on *The Honey Badger*, by Robert Ruark. This vivid portrait of a suave 1950s literary cad finds the author's self-important alter-ego, Alec Barr, gliding through life with enviable ease and panache.

WINTER 2000

LOST AND FOUND
[CONTINUED]

86 Robert Polito on Michael Edwards' *Priscilla, Elvis and Me: In the Shadow of the King*. In his memoir, Edwards—a vainglorious ex-model and former Priscilla Presley boy toy—proves that his obsession with the King is as grand as his obsession with himself.

88 John Frederick Moore dusts off David Bradley's 1981 PEN/Faulkner Award winner *The Chaneysville Incident*, which tells the powerful story of a black historian on a quest to uncover the buried evil of his hometown.

90 Sallie Tisdale on Robert Paul Smith's *Where Did You Go? Out. What Did You Do? Nothing*. The charming, pitch-perfect 1958 children's classic is still as sharp and relevant as the day it was written.

92 Eddie Little lauds Alex Abella's *The Killing of the Saints*. Raymond Chandler with a Latin beat, this fast-paced, hard-boiled mystery follows two Cuban practitioners of Santeria accused of a cold-blooded massacre in Los Angeles's Hispanic community.

A READABLE FEAST

184 Sara Perry • THE APPLE OF THEIR EYES
Sara Perry finds that Jane Austen, Alice B. Toklas, and Erskine Caldwell all baked a mean apple pie.

THE LAST WORD

196 Benjamin Anastas • SICK ART
The author is truly revolted by art from around the world.

---

34 PORTFOLIO: Desert Citizens, by Mark Klett, continued on pp. 110-111, 130-131, and 182-183

202 The Literary Crostic, by John M. Daniel

204 CONTRIBUTORS

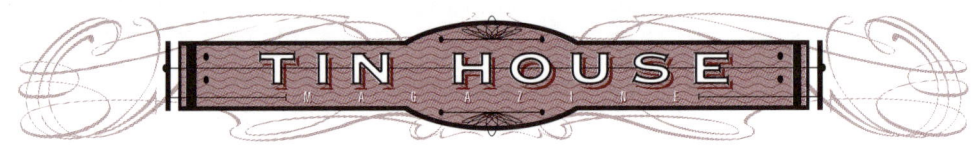

Editor-in-Chief/Publisher
WIN MCCORMACK

. . . .

Editors
ROB SPILLMAN AND ELISSA SCHAPPELL

Managing Editor
HOLLY MACARTHUR

Senior Editor
TUCKER MALARKEY

Poetry Editor
AMY BARTLETT

Editor-at-Large
JEANNE MCCULLOCH

Assistant Editor
SERENA CRAWFORD

Editorial Assistant
CHRISTINA CHIU

Contributing Editors
AGHA SHAHID ALI • DOROTHY ALLISON • ALBERTO FUGUET
CHRISTOPHER MERRILL • RICK MOODY
HELEN SCHULMAN • TOM SPANBAUER • IRVINE WELSH

Photo Consultant
RANDY GRAGG

Art Director
JON BAIRD

Copy Editor
GREG VILLEPIQUE

. . . .

Tin House is published quarterly by McCormack Communications. Vol. 1, No.3, Winter 2000. Printed by Edwards Brothers, Ann Arbor, MI. Basic subscription price: 1 year $39.80. Send subscriptions requests or manuscript submissions (with SASE) to: P.O. Box 10500, Portland, OR 97296-0500. ©1999 McCormack Communications LLC. All rights reserved. Neither this publication nor any part of it may be reproduced, stored in a retrieval system, or transmitted in any form or by any means, electronic, mechanical, photocopying, recording or otherwise, without the prior written permission of McCormack Communications LLC. Tin House™, Tin House Magazine and Design™, New Voices™, Profiles™, Pilgrimage™, Lost and Found™, A Readable Feast™, The Last Word™, Literary Personals™ and the Design Only of the various drawings of Houses throughout this periodical are trademarks or service marks of McCormack Communications LLC.

THE BOOK REVIEW FOR ART, FICTION & CULTURE WINTER 1999 $3.00

BOOKFORUM

**Greil Marcus on
NOIR STYLE**

**David Toop on
SOUND IN ART**

**Dale Peck interviews
SUSAN SONTAG**

**Francine Prose on
CARSON McCULLERS**

**Gordon Grice on
NABOKOV'S BUTTERFLIES**

PLUS reviews by Arthur C. Danto, Daniel Mendelsohn, Jonathan Lethem, Paul West, Amy Hempel, Michael FitzGerald, Jim Lewis, Lee Smith, Erik Davis, and more

DON'T GET CAUGHT WITHOUT IT

Subscribe 1 800-783 4903 and save 50% off the cover price

8 issues (2 years) of Bookforum at the special rate of $12
When calling please refer to #312993

beach town

new fiction from
Amy Hempel

The house next door was rented for the summer to a couple who swore at missed croquet shots. Their music at night was loud, and I liked it; it was not music I knew. Mornings, I picked up the empties they had lobbed across the hedge, Coronas with the limes wedged inside, and pitched them back over. We had not introduced ourselves these three months.

Between our houses a tall privet hedge is backed by white pine for privacy in winter. The day I heard the voice of a woman not the wife, I went out back to a spot more heavily planted but with a break I could just see through. Now it was the man who was talking, or trying to—he started to say things he could not seem to finish. I watched the woman do something memorable to him with her mouth. Then the man pulled her up from where she had been kneeling. He said, "Maybe you're just hungry. Maybe we should get you something to eat."

The woman had a nimble laugh.

The man said, "Paris is where you and I should go."

The woman asked what was wrong with here. She said, "I like a beach town."

I wanted to phone the wife's office in the city and hear what she would sound like if she answered. I had no fellow feeling; all she had ever said to me was couldn't I mow my lawn later in the day. It was noon when she asked. I told her the village bylaws disallow mowing before seven-thirty, and that I had waited until nine. A gardener, hired by my neighbor, cared for their yard. But still I was sure they were neglecting my neighbor's orchids. All summer long I had watched for the renters to leave the house together so that I could let myself in with the key from the shelf in the shed and test the soil and water the orchids.

The woman who did not want to go to Paris said that she had to leave. "But I don't *want* you to leave," the man said, and she said, "Think of the kiss at the door."

Nobody thinks about the way sound carries across water. Even the water in a swimming pool. A week later, when her husband was away, the wife had friends to lunch by the pool. I didn't have to hide to listen; I was in view if they had cared to look, pulling weeds in the raspberry canes.

The women told the wife it was an opportunity for her. They said fair is fair, and to do those things she might not otherwise have done. "No regrets," they said, "if you are even the type of person who is given to regret, if you even have that type of wistful temperament to begin with."

The woman said, "We are not unintelligent; we just let passion prevail." They said, "Who would deny that we have all had these feelings?"

The women told the wife she would not feel this way forever. "You will feel worse, however, before you feel better, and that is just the way it always is."

The women advised long walks. They told the wife to watch the sun rise and set, to look for solace in the natural world, though they admitted there *was* no comfort to be found in the world and they would all be fools to expect it.

The weekend the couple next door moved in—their rental began on Memorial Day—I heard them place a bet on the moon. She said waxing, he said waning. Days later, the moon nearly full in the night sky, I listened for the woman to tell her husband she had won, knowing they had not named the terms of the bet, and that the woman next door would collect nothing.

CRUELCITIES

JONATHAN NAPACK PROFILES CHINA'S "POSTER CHILD FOR SPIRITUAL POLLUTION,"

MIAN MIAN

I. SHENZHEN, MAY 1997

"This place has no history," Judy says. "You don't know what that means. For Chinese. To be free from history."

She is tall and ivory-skinned and from Beijing. The music throbs as lights spin and eddy over the dance floor. This club used to be a theater, part of a People's Liberation Army garrison. Fifteen years ago, troops here watched "model revolutionary operas." Now they work as bouncers.

We dance for a while, then take a break outside. The air is still sultry, hours before dawn. Ragged-looking flower hawkers squat on the curbside as kebab smoke drifts in and out with the breeze. We find a quiet corner to sit down. She rolls up her sleeves and rests her arm inside mine. I look at the jangly Japanese watch, blue glass, white metal, dangling from her wrist. She says she finished her first year at university and smiles a clear, bright northern smile. "Maybe I'll find a job here."

Shiftless kids with hennaed hair loiter on the steps, checking out the pretty girls. Chinese discos feel so different. It's the electricity of discovering pleasure for the first time. The sky gleams with steel and glass. Broken bottles litter the sidewalk.

This city is so strange. Five million people where fifteen years ago was nothing but paddies and buffalo. At night, the border glows like a twisting, burning fuse, separating downtown Shenzhen from Hong Kong's rural New Territories, the lakes, mountains, and fjords of Plover Cove. To get here, you take a train to that border. You cross a bridge spanning a fetid river, where British soldiers stand on one side, Chinese on the other. A clock counts down the seconds to July 1, 1997, and a sign promises *Hong Kong Will Have a More B autif l Future*.

Shenzhen is already the bizarro-world Hong Kong. The icons of first-world consumerism are there—Starbucks, McDonald's, Chanel—but twisted, displaced. Cocktail waitresses wear Santa Claus costumes in steamy weather; light boxes tout face lifts from unlicensed surgeons; bent-over migrants from faraway provinces beg outside Kmart. In a hotel driveway, a BMW with government plates sports a rear-window sticker from the New York Athletic Club.

It is China's dream of the future. And its nightmare. Across the street, under a rubble-strewn underpass, a pack of hungry-looking boys try to sell a young girl. "Xiaojie! Xiaojie!" they hiss.

No older than twelve, I guess; slim hips, flat chest. She stands in soiled silk pajamas and, bravely, tries to smile.

I think of something I read in the newspaper. "Selling my body," a prostitute explained, "is easier than selling vegetables."

"What are you thinking?" Judy says. I laugh and say nothing. We stay like that for a while, half embarrassed, half entranced. Then she writes her pager number on my hand and disappears inside.

II.

"There are no old people in that city," Mian Mian says of Shenzhen. "Everyone is so young."

We meet at Goya, a murky, loungey kind of bar in Shanghai's old French Concession. Sinking into cozy crushed-velvet chairs, we order a nutritious meal of peanuts and dry martinis and shoot the breeze.

CRUEL CITIES: AN INTERVIEW WITH MIAN MIAN

Mian Mian is the *nom de guerre* of Shen Wang, the twenty-nine-year-old from Shanghai who is China's most visible chronicler of the country's disaffected youth and also one of China's most promising young writers. Her willingness to embrace taboo subjects like drugs and sexuality, particularly female sexuality, have made her into a popular phenomenon, a cult hero on the mainland, where her books have been quietly but prolifically published, pirated by street vendors, and snatched up by tens of thousands of young readers eager for her straightforward, transgressive writing.

Despite Mian Mian's fame, many Chinese have never read her books.

Mian Mian at 25

Mian Mian with club-kid friends in Shanghai

the media, as a symbol rather than an author.

Her visibility marks the emergence of a generation that has known only the corrupt quasi-capitalism of the post-1989 era, a generation that grew up with Nirvana, not Lei Feng. Mian Mian is the poster child of what the hardline communists have dubbed "Spiritual Pollution."

She looks alarmingly apt for the role. Tall and lanky in a regulation black dress, with lacquered bangs over big, deep eyes, she smokes incessantly, adding to her seductive whiskey voice. Moodily veering between lachrymose gloom and mischievous high spirits, she travels with a movable feast of pals like the fey deejay Coco and her trippy assistant Casper, a former nurse.

She was born Shen Wang in Shanghai. Her father, a famous engineer, made sure she attended an elite school for university-bound students. But at fourteen, something went wrong.

"Suddenly I changed," she says. "I

Censorship in China is murkier than it used to be, with gray areas which expand and contract depending on the mood in Zhongnanhai. The publishing industry is fragmented into thousands of small publishers printing runs of five thousand or less. Distribution is primitive, with most books sold by street vendors and kiosks. Although publishers themselves remain cautious, the vendors are less so, and they openly sell controversial books—such as pirated copies of Mian Mian's Hong Kong editions. Many people know Mian Mian only from stopped doing homework. I questioned everything. I thought a lot about sex, and wanted to find out more. But there was nowhere I could turn to." Two years later, a classmate tried to kill herself and was institutionalized. "Until then, I thought I was uniquely weird."

Her teenage years coincided with the "culture fever" of the mid-1980s. The liberal rule of Premier Hu Yaobang had an electric effect on a society finally recovered from the trauma of the 1970s and Mao Zedong's political and cultural experiments. Individualism and experimentation flourished for the first time since 1949. The "opening up" policy also meant that rock music and other products of Western pop culture became available.

The book that opened her eyes was by Xu Xing, one of the post-Cultural Revolution "modernists" who reintroduced irony, sarcasm, and black humor into mainland fiction. "It was so lonely, and extremely dark," she says, "but also funny and very sensitive." Inspired by her classmate's suicide attempt and a Madonna video seen on a popular TV program sponsored by Nescafé, she wrote "Like a Prayer," which she considers (false starts aside) her "real" first story. "This one was already really my style. I was so young then, and my heart was so dark," she laments.

She submitted the story to *Shanghai Wenxue*, China's most famous literary journal at the time. She was thrilled by the response. On accepting the story, the editor told Mian Mian, "China is filled with writers who write one short story. You have to write another." Dreaming of fame as a novelist, she dropped out of high school.

However, it was not to be. Deng Xiaoping's 1987 ouster of the too-liberal Hu led to a cooling in the cultural climate, prefiguring the deep freeze of two years

> ON ACCEPTING THE STORY, THE EDITOR TOLD MIAN MIAN, "CHINA IS FILLED WITH WRITERS WHO WRITE ONE SHORT STORY. YOU HAVE TO WRITE ANOTHER."

later. The magazine changed its mind. "They said teenage suicide was too controversial," she remembers bitterly. "They were afraid of the government."

"I was shaken," she says. "I thought I had no chance in this world. I had no education, no job, nothing, The only thing in my life was writing, and I failed at that. There was only one thing left. I could make money.

"So I went to Shenzhen."

III.
BEIJING, OCTOBER 1999

Tanks. Stone. Frost. Bicycles.

This is China the way the world sees it.

Grainy TV images, pixels lost somewhere on the vastness of Tiananmen Square. "New" China's fiftieth birthday.

President Jiang, Mao-suited and rotund, waves to the parade. A women's militia goose-steps in pink miniskirts and patent-leather boots. Childlike model rockets celebrate "modernity." Jiang sucks in air, turns red, and bursts out, in that peculiar, accordionlike way of aged cadres, "Comrades, are you working hard?"

A student says, "I hope foreigners can see this parade, so they'll be impressed and invest in our country."

Another jokes, "Do you think if I jumped in front of the tanks, I'd become a hero like that guy?"

If capitals are semiotic landscapes, Beijing is a minefield. It is like a theme park of discredited ideologies. A center that is not a center. Founded by Mongols, built up by Manchus, reinstated by Communists. Capital of oppressive foreign dynasties.

Mike Davies's *Ecology of Fear*, which portrays Los Angeles's disaster-prone ecology as the incarnation of its dysfunctional society, might as well have been written about Beijing as Los Angeles. Dust storms, mud rain, temperatures that seesaw from heatstroke to frostbite with barely a spring or autumn between—there have even been plagues of locusts, a result of Mao's decision to kill all sparrows.

Isolation is inscribed in architecture. Walls make the Chinese worldview incarnate. China's ancient cities barricade themselves against the world, as if afraid of experiencing it: Nanjing turns its back on the Yangzi, Hangzhou ignores the ocean in favor of its tidy, domestic West Lake. How different are the nineteenth-century treaty ports—Dalian, Qingdao, Hong Kong—facing out toward their harbors.

On the street, nerves rubbed raw. Greasy food and smoky cars. Grubby winter cabbages and green summer melons. The reek of mutton fat, so uncommon in China—yet another Mongol influence. That soft whirring Beijing *r*, swallowing whole words

CRUEL CITIES: AN INTERVIEW WITH MIAN MIAN

in Gobi dust. A sense of seething. Of anger.

The Australian sinologist W. F. Jenner once wrote, "[China's] history of tyranny is matched by the tyranny of history—an imperialism of the mind that finds self-affirmation in the subjection of others."

Beijing is saturated with this legacy. June 4th evoked the symbols of Western democracy, but did many understand "democracy" to mean the right of the intelligentsia to steer the nation's destiny? Even Su Xiakang's reformist television series *Heshang* ("Yellow River Elegy") still imagined scholars "irrigating the yellow earth with the fresh sweet spring of science and democracy."

Perhaps the true opposition lay among the despised merchants of the south. During more than a thousand years of persecution, they forged an identity in exile of laissez-faire and seagoing trade, a strategy of noncompliance embodied in their motto: The mountains are high, the Emperor is far away.

Mian Mian in front of a Shanghai sex shop

In the south, anyone could make it. Money conquered all. Against autocracy, the ultimate weapon. Best summed up by Taiwanese President Lee Teng-hui, who once declared, referring to the Chinese national hero on Taiwan's one-hundred-dollar note, "We will conquer the world with Sun Yat-sen."

IV.

"I stayed there seven years," Mian Mian says. "They were the most important of my life."

When she arrived in 1987, Shenzhen had only existed for three years. Deng Xiaoping had founded it as a kind of economic experiment. But the city became something more. China was then still more than nominally socialist—the government assigned jobs and work units still ruled people's lives. Shenzhen's free labor market was unique in China, and it became a place of experimentation, where people tried to redefine themselves, a kind of laboratory of individualism.

It was also brutal. The result of unleashing a generation whose foundational experience was making their parents kneel on broken glass was not pretty. "That city is so sick. Everyone just thinks of themselves. A lot of lost people came there. They dreamed of using money to save their lives."

In 1987, Shenzhen was already booming. Even without a high-school degree, one could find plenty of jobs. But by the early nineties, things went to another level. Deng's 1992 visit set loose another round of reforms. The *maquiledoras* moved further into the Pearl River delta and Shenzhen morphed into a glitzy service hub, part Las Vegas, part Cayman Islands. As a kind of exotic offshore banking center, it laundered heroin profits and stolen cars for triad societies. Drugs were everywhere, as were girls from "up north" who came to sell their only possession: their bodies.

This boom transformed China. June 4th destroyed any hopes about the cruel and stupid regime. But even if you couldn't buck the system, you could opt out by going into business—*xiahai* (literally, "dive into the sea"). As other cities followed Shenzhen down the yellow brick road, something

> **THE RESULT OF UNLEASHING A GENERATION WHOSE FOUNDATIONAL EXPERIENCE WAS MAKING THEIR PARENTS KNEEL ON BROKEN GLASS WAS NOT PRETTY.**

changed. People started taking responsibility for their lives. This new world was tacky and charmless, but it was theirs. The Party fed off it, but as parasites, not creators.

We order another round of martinis. Mian Mian turns over in her chair, one arm propped against the cushions, her legs dangling from the armrest. "That city is so cruel. It has no heart. But those seven years were also very real. It made me think about what human beings are really like."

"I fell in love there. He was a singer. Just a nightclub singer. But I saw something more in him. He was so talented. I was so in love with him. And there we were, together in that cruel city."

He betrayed her, she moved out. A friend introduced her to heroin. She liked it. "I just wanted to sleep."

"I didn't know what danger is," she reflects. "And I didn't know what freedom is. I did whatever I wanted. I felt very powerful, but I still couldn't find any love. No one is your friend in that city."

Mian Mian's father was getting rich himself, engineering China's mushrooming infrastructure. Out of misplaced guilt, he started sending her money, and she plunged into full-scale addiction.

"For three years, I never left my room. I did no work. I never answered the phone. I forgot rock 'n' roll. I forgot I ever was a writer. I only remembered my parents." She lights a Zhongnanhai cigarette, takes a deep drag, and leans back. "Because they gave me money.

Heroin is super fucking rubbish."

Every night she stayed up watching *cheung pin*—remaindered back-catalogue films used as filler by Hong Kong television, society comedies and Cantonese operas from the black-and-white era. For Mian Mian, their flickering light felt like some kind of calm radiating over the airwaves. "They were the only thing that made me feel relaxed. That made me feel like a human being."

"You know, that city has no history, so I inscribed it with my own. Everything I did became its history."

V.
SHANGHAI, FEBRUARY 1999

This is a city of ghosts.

Shanghai wears its shabby European ruins like a threadbare Savile Row suit. Its muted colors look chiaroscuro, all tungsten glow and marshland gray-indigo, amber, cinnabar. In Frenchtown, winter is cold and windswept. Dead leaves rattle the plane trees arching over the avenues.

It's the sadness of paths not taken. This was China's first marvelous, tragic stab at modernity, its attempt to break out and find *der Weg ins Freie,* as Arthur Schnitzler put it, "the way into the open." In the 1930's, it was a cosmopolis embracing both a lively Chinese avant-garde and legions of Jewish

and Russian refugees. Its studios rivaled Hollywood's. Its industries readied for greatness.

But Shanghai never made it. The Communists demolished what little survived the war. The foreigners went home. The tycoons and film stars decamped to Hong Kong. And now, like Berlin, Shanghai talks about recreating a lost past without having any human connection to it. Nostalgia. If the Cantonese are nouveaux riches, then you might call the Shanghainese nouveaux pauvres.

The city's amour propre proved remarkably resilient. "China is open now" is the mantra on everyone's lips, but despite its pride Shanghai makes do with hand-me-downs—last season's clothing lines, pirated copies of third-rate Hollywood movies. It sees the world with its nose pressed to the glass.

Yet Shanghai remains haunted. Its ghosts refuse to give up. The writer Xu Zhimo, for example, represents everything China could have been—refined, tolerant, open to the world. Xu studied at Cambridge, and traveled widely; his acquaintances ranged from Bertrand Russell and Thomas Hardy to Rabindranath Tagore and Paul Cézanne. He moved to Shanghai in 1927, where he formed the *Xinyuehui*, or "Crescent Moon Society," which tried to carve out a space for imaginative freedom in an increasingly inhumane China. He died in a plane crash four years later.

Shanghai is saturated with such memories, but, unlike Beijing's, they inspire rather than oppress. Maybe the way out is still there. To merely free oneself from history is to acknowledge Beijing's mastery of it. Maybe there is still time to avoid the grim fate Mao himself foretold: *Kaichu qiuji*. "Expelled from the human race."

VI.

"Finally I went home to Shanghai," Mian Mian says. "My dad told me I could take all their money and never see them again. Or I could go to the hospital.

"I chose the hospital."

Rehab in China uses crude but effective forms of aversion therapy. In Mian Mian's case, they put her in a ward for the criminally insane. "It was such a horrible memory," she says. "I never took drugs again."

When she left in 1995, she was still just twenty-five. She lived at home, spending her days watching movies on her VCR. After a while, she started to write again, stories which she later gathered into her book *La La La*. "All the editors said they loved it, but it had to change, there was too much drugs. But I didn't want to change it. So I wrote stories, just as a game, for magazines. These made me well-known in China by the time I published *La La La* in 1997 in Hong Kong."

La La La quickly seeped back to the mainland. A series of four interlocking stories, it spoke of love, music, drugs, and despair in Shenzhen, a combination that remarkably resembled her own life. Her prose was hypnotic, rhythmic, staccato like her native Shanghainese, evoking the persistent, driving beat of the music that informed her vision.

Mian Mian's life changed drastically. As she became famous, she started organizing parties for new Chinese music (using her English name, Kika). She became a staple of gossip columns fixated on her love life, real and imagined. Once a Shenzhen acquaintance even used events from her life to write a book purporting to be hers.

She says she loathes the attention. "They printed all these lies about my life. I felt like a fake. For a while, I stopped writing."

That proved shortlived, and this year she published *Candy,* her first full-length novel, and two short stories: "One Patient," inspired by her time at the hospital, and "Your Night, My Day," about her experiences in Shenzhen, which she says she will expand into her next novel. "My message is, this world is cruel," she says, "but if you believe in beautiful things, you can survive."

After finishing *Candy,* she embarked upon a series of promotional parties in Chinese cities—Shenzhen, Chengdu, Guangzhou—with deejays and new Chinese bands. "My book is not for intellectuals," she explains. "My readers are in the disco, bar, rock concert, in the street."

This differs markedly from the role Chinese writers usually arrogate to themselves. "I don't want to teach anybody," she insists. "I just want to show them my life. A lot of young people are getting lost. I want to tell them of my experience. I want to show them how freedom is exciting, but also dangerous."

It's getting late. We are all a little drunk. A gust of wind blows the door open. I ask her to describe herself.

"Kika is a party queen. Mian Mian is a writer. And Shen Wang is a sad, complicated person with a lot of secrets."

An Excerpt from Candy by Mian Mian

Translated by Serena Crawford

One morning in December of 1994, I went out to buy water. God knows how I drifted toward a small, slow-moving car. My head and my right eye were injured. The nurse shaved off my long head of hair. During the course of surgery on my eye, all the anesthesia wore off.

My father came to this city. He thanked the car accident for letting him know I was still doing drugs.

Once again, my father put me in the Shanghai Drug Clinic.

Before I returned to Shanghai, San Mao gave me a big pile of all kinds of hats. He said, This is fate. I feel you're going to get better. See, you look good in hats.

Carrying six large, full suitcases, my father and I arrived at the airport. I hid the drugs in my underwear because I constantly had to feed my addiction. My father didn't understand this.

Going through airport inspection, I nervously watched my father. I thought: He's a good person, I'm a bad person.

The moment the plane took off, I fucking cried. I swore never to return to this city again.

My nurse came to ask me what I wanted to eat one evening. She said, You have some sesame rice

AN EXCERPT FROM 'CANDY'

balls and some Chef Kang instant noodles. Next, she said, Do you want to wash your face? Do you need me to give you a little hot water? I opened my eyes to see this person standing by the side of my bed. She was a woman over the age of forty with big cheekbones. Her cheekbones jutted out. Her face was dark and red. She wore deep red cotton clothes and pants. She looked like a common laborer. I said, Why are you my nurse? Why is everyone here wearing the same clothes except for me? She said, Because I am a patient. I said, You also came to quit drugs? Her mouth opened slowly. She said, You don't know what sickness patients here have? I said, What sickness? This is a drug clinic, isn't it? Her body swayed back and forth. She kindly told me, We are all mentally ill people who have made mistakes. I said, What? Mentally ill people? What mistake did you make? Her eyes looked at my eyes. She said, I killed my husband's father. I said, Killed him? Why did you kill him? She said, Because he was always cursing me, so I put some pesticide in his food.

I am a drug addict. I am every mother's nightmare. I devoted myself to alcohol and music. Then I dedicated myself to heroin and chocolate. Then I thought I was born addicted to chemicals. I always thought in this respect I was a solitary lunatic. This afternoon I was brought here by my father. Now, my reflexes are especially slow because I have already taken the medicine. I think my mind isn't clear, but I am still scared by what is happening. I think the Communist Party (my father) is really severe, taking drug addicts and insane people who are murderers and putting them together for treatment. This way when patients who have quit drugs leave, they won't want to do drugs again. Compared to them, I think I should be ashamed of my behavior; I have already started to feel ashamed. Heroin has turned me into an idiot. When I came in the afternoon, I wondered why there was only me in this room, why Shanghai's drug addicts were so old.

Within the most unbearable seventy-two hours, because of my extreme case of asthma, the doctor doesn't "sedate" me. Every day my nurse helps me go to the bathroom, wash my face, brush my teeth. She also cleans my room for me. One time when she is helping me go to the bathroom, a patient says to me, Look at the state you're in now. When you leave don't do drugs again, you know?

This is a very big room. Inside this big room is another big room. It's the sleeping room of the mentally insane and the violent drug addicts. It looks like there are countless beds. A snow-white blanket is arranged on each bed. These blankets look like magazines, I even think of those underground books of Beijing. There is also a room with a toilet and a sink. It's always dark in there except for a thread of moonlight. During the day, the rays of light also seem like moonlight, as cold as an ice willow. In the smallest room, there are four bunk beds. It's the room for drug addicts who are willing to quit on their own.

In the sunshine, the patients make playing cards or pull their clothes apart. They chat. Sometimes they chat with the doctor. They sound like small birds. I watch them from my room. Everything looks peaceful. After lunch they sing, all together they sing. This is their required homework. Besides singing "The Gold Mountain of Beijing Shines in All Directions," this kind of old song, they also sing some modern songs, for example "Xiao Sa Zou Yi Hui," "Thank You for Your Love." These songs are copied on the small blackboard and taught to them by the drug addicts continually coming and going. After they sing, they get in line to receive medicine and then take naps.

All the hormones make me look like an idiot. The patients over there in the sunlight make playing cards. The big door is locked. In this way, losing control of one's life is almost real, like the winter of this ice-cold city concealing a murderer's motive. My mind is continually empty. I don't think this is because of the medicine. Every time I've stopped after

> **THE BIG DOOR IS LOCKED. IN THIS WAY, LOSING CONTROL OF ONE'S LIFE IS ALMOST REAL, LIKE THE WINTER OF THIS ICE-COLD CITY CONCEALING A MURDERER'S MOTIVE.**

An Excerpt From 'Candy'

repeatedly taking drugs every day, I can't find the meaning in my life. After I'm disconnected from the IV, I start going out to the big room to sit in the sun. Suddenly there is a patient by my side who bumps me. She says, Give me a cracker, okay? She looks away. From time to time she turns to watch me look for a cracker. When I give her the cracker, a lot of patients watch me. But they quickly withdraw their gazes. I suddenly realize all of the patients have the habit of swaying their bodies. At the same time they sway their bodies, they shift their feet.

I am permitted to call my father. I say, *Baba*, I'm good. It's just that I want a mirror, they took my mirror away. I thought they would still give me a mirror. I want a mirror. My doctor calls me into the office. She says, I didn't give you a mirror because I was afraid you would kill yourself, or other patients would take it and there would be a disaster. Now, put it away for yourself.

This evening a patient in the bathroom shyly says to me, Can you give me the mirror to use for a moment? Just for a moment? I'll give it right back. I look at her. I say, Just for five minutes, okay? I take out my palm-sized mirror. Everyone starts to take turns looking in the mirror. This evening I am not lonely in the slightest. The one who asked me for the mirror looks at herself the longest. A patient tells me she is still a virgin, she's already been here fifteen years. I say, No wonder you look so young. She says she's not young, old, old. When she says old, old, my eyes start to tear. Quitting drugs, it's easy to cry, sometimes it's incomprehensible. I'm a little embarrassed about crying but no one notices. To cover up my embarrassment, I quickly ask, How did you get here? A patient tells me this person committed assault. She killed all of her sister's children. I say, God! God! She touches her face in the mirror. A patient says She says they were devils. So she killed them. A patient says, Because her sister wasn't good to her.

I take back my mirror. That evening I continually think about why there are people who go crazy to the point of murder. Why weren't they taken to the hospital before that? In the moonlight, I think, I'm very lucky. I suddenly am certain I am not a chemical freak. I am just a person who is as scared as a mouse, or as my father says, My daughter is definitely a good child. She's just lost her way.

My meals are the same as the other patients'. It's food I really have no way of swallowing. I can tell the doctor to buy small wrapped packages of food for me in the small hospital store. My nurse cooks food for me every day. Every time I want to give her food to eat, but so far she hasn't eaten, except when the doctor tells her to eat. Then she eats. A patient tells me her family has never come to see her because she killed her husband's father. They also don't pay for her treatment. So every day, besides being a nurse, she also goes out in galoshes to a restaurant to make a living. I think she really likes to work. It makes her seem happy. A patient laughs and tells me she only makes enough money to pay the bare minimum expenses. She has no money to buy toilet paper, buy soap. She always takes a sheet of toilet paper into the bathroom. When she squats down she hides the toilet paper in her pocket.

A patient stands there facing the wall. I realize she's the "virgin patient." I stand next to her. She looks down, doesn't look at me. A patient tells me she's being punished again. Once again, because she's mentally ill, she claimed the hospital director was her husband.

A patient is called into the office. I hear the warden ask her, What did you steal from the drug-addict patients? Then she keeps repeating, Mustard apple banana banana apple mustard.

The time for me to leave finally comes. While I'm thanking everybody, I tell my father to give the doctor a hundred dollars. I say this money is for my nurse to buy things, to thank her for her help.

The second time my father takes me back to this hospital, I'm bald. High on drugs and in a daze, I'm hit by a car. I lose my long hair and I am thinner than thin. I think I myself am unable to recognize myself.

I never thought when I passed the big iron lock of the sick ward, a patient would yell out my name. She says, She's come again, she's come again, this time she has no hair.

This time my father says again, My daughter is definitely a good child, she's just too uninhibited. For this we are responsible, we are willing to pay the price. The doctor says, We are all moved by your father. Think about it yourself. Then I'm sent to be tested for HIV and syphilis. Then the doctor gives me medicine. This time they don't give me the same medicine as last time. They switch the method of treatment. They say, We have to make you suffer, otherwise you'll never change.

Every day I have some yellow, pink, and white pills. When I take this medicine, I have no way of sleeping. My whole body is feverish. I pace back and forth in my room. Sometimes, I talk to myself nonstop, disconnected and jumbled. One evening, a patient suddenly slips into my room. She says, If you want to get out of here, don't take the yellow pills again. When I look up she's gone. She scared me. After I cry for a while, I decide not to take the yellow pills. I tell the doctor I do not want to take the yellow pills.

After having a lot of nightmares, I gradually get better once again. This time, I start to work with the others. A patient teaches me how to make cards. I start to miss my mother, the food she cooked. I miss everything about her. I look at the blackboard and sing songs with them every day, it's just that I can't stand the food. Once a month there is braised meat for lunch. This is when the patients are happiest. A patient says, Why aren't you eating the meat? Why don't you eat meat? The doctor overhears her. My doctor is a very pretty woman from Shanghai. She's a stylish intellectual. She says, Why don't you eat this meat? I say, I feel nauseous. Really nauseous. She says, Who do you think you are? Today, I want you to eat it. I say, I really can't eat it. She says, Do you want to get out of here? I say yes. She says, Then eat. There is no difference between you and the other patients, you need to remember this. I say, I won't eat. She says, Okay, I'll call your father, then we'll see if you'll eat. Then she watches me eat that piece of meat, and watches me vomit it up in fits. I cry and vomit at the same time. She says, You are the same as the other patients. Don't let me see you waste food again. Your nurse never received the hundred dollars you gave her. Did you know that? There is no difference between you and the other patients. Furthermore, because of you she can never be a nurse again. Remember this.

A patient gets a skin disease so she can't work with us. She sits alone on a wooden stool and watches us work. When I pass by her, she asks me, When you were outside, where did you *hun*? I say, What? What's that? Where did you *hun*? She says, At JJ's disco. Then she looks at me. She doesn't look like a sick person at all, but she also has that habit of swaying her body, constantly shifting her feet.

A group of drug addicts is brought in by a police car. It starts to get a little noisy. They are violent drug addicts. One time a patient suddenly says to me, Your veins are so good, not the smallest problem. Inserting the needle must be very pleasant. Suddenly, I think, *There is no difference between you and the other patients,* these words. I take shelter back in my room.

Near the end of the year, the patients are taken to Pudong in a pretty bus. When we return, a patient says to me, You know, it's very nice outside now.

> YOUR VEINS ARE SO GOOD, NOT THE SMALLEST PROBLEM. INSERTING THE NEEDLE MUST BE VERY PLEASANT.

HOW DO YOU KNOW THESE SONGS? SHE SAYS, I'M A TEACHER. I SAY, WHY ARE YOU HERE? SHE SAYS, I KILLED MY HUSBAND.

Over Christmas, we have our own party. A patient eats my chocolate and starts to sing a song for everybody to hear. She is the only patient here who wears glasses. She sings Christmas songs. She sings without restraint, blending true and false, her high pitch is exquisite. After she finishes singing, I ask her, How do you know these songs? She says, I'm a teacher. I say, Why are you here? She says, I killed my husband. I say, Why did you kill your husband? She says, He was too small, one strangle and I strangled him to death. After she says this, she has a peaceful expression on her face.

I start to hate myself. I think heroin has ruined my mind. Otherwise, why do I think I have the right to ask them, "Why are you here?"

I swear I'll never ask this question again.

That day, we assemble to sing a little love song. Several dozen old women loudly sing, "Let me think of you think of you think of you, think of you for the last time, because tomorrow I will become somebody else's bride, think deeply of you." The song is sung neatly, without emotion, but still it moves me, touches my heart. The first time I find my heart.

In the days after, I often run into this song. I know it's called "Language of the Heart." Each time I come across this song, I suddenly break down. I stop whatever I'm doing and listen until it ends. This song reminds me of where I'm from.

The morning after Christmas, I wake up very early. A patient comes into my room to take my bowl. She asks me, Why aren't you eating this good steamed bun? Every day she asks me the same question, every day I answer, I don't want it, you eat it. This day after I finish speaking she takes my bowl and leaves. Then she gets a mop and comes back in and prepares to mop the floor. Then she suddenly leans against the wall and spits up a white froth and curls up around herself. I'm too afraid to yell. I look at her. I look at my heater. I'm scared she'll suddenly pick up the heater and beat me. Just then the nurse walks by. I lower

AN EXCERPT FROM 'CANDY'

my voice and say, Look, what's the matter with her? After the nurse comes in, she takes the mop and puts it in her hand, lets her hold onto it. She says to her, Everything will be all right. It's nothing, it will be all right. A couple of minutes later she gets up and continues to mop the floor. Her face is white, her hair like steel wire. I want to go over and mop the floor, but I'm too frightened to move. After a moment, the nurse comes in and says to me, She was sick because she ate your bun. She eats your bun every day. Today she was criticized by a group of patients so she got sick. In the future, if you don't eat your bun, please take turns giving it to each of them.

When the time is almost up, everybody cleans themselves and dresses up because visiting time has come. A patient eats cake together with her son. A patient talks with her husband. A patient is together with her mother, her mother is unbelievably old. Over there a patient waits. I sit on the edge of my bed, both hands stuck in my sleeves. Both of my feet sway. I look at the chocolate my mother has given me. My mother sat in my room for only ten minutes. She said, The guard at the door is cruel. She said, The guard said you drug addicts are worthless. My mother said she felt like a criminal so she quickly had to leave, she couldn't bear listening to this again.

When the time to leave gets closer, I am put in the big room with all the other patients. Every night they talk in their dreams. I can't sleep, always hungry. In the middle of the night I gnaw on crackers. A patient watches me from under her blanket and laughs. She says, I can't imagine why you're sleeping in here.

I go home. I say, I want to shower, I haven't had a shower in a long time. I say, The shower in the house is too cold. I'm scared of cold. I want to go to the public shower. My mother gives me one dollar, she says it's enough. I think she doesn't dare give me more money because she's afraid I'll go buy drugs.

I return to the town where I was born. I go to the public shower where I went often as a child. I wear the wig my father bought for me. I am out of breath as I shower. Because I don't have any strength left, my wig falls off. There is a person who first looks at my wig and then looks at my woolly head. Finally, her gaze rests on my body.

After the shower, I use twenty cents to buy a piece of fried *ci fan gao*. The *ci fan gao* rolls in my mouth, sticks to my teeth. I think, this *ci fan gao* is so delicious and cheap. I'm so happy I don't have to eat Chef Kang and Xian Qu crackers. I think, I do not want to eat those things again in my lifetime. I think, Perhaps at this moment my life can start over. I think of my family. I think, Now I am not cold. I think of the hospital I just left. I think, I am now the only patient who has gotten out for the New Year. Then I tell myself: Really, heroin is high-grade trash.

PORTFOLIO

MARK KLETT'S

... Desert Citizens *portrays saguaro cacti, many of which live to be over two hundred years old. Taken in the Sonoran Desert of southern Arizona and northern Mexico, these photographs were inspired by the local Tohono O'Odham tribe's belief that the cacti are inhabited by the souls of their ancestors. But the images are also part of Klett's career-long effort to create a landscape photography that "breaks down the barriers between self and place."*

A native New Yorker, Klett was trained as a geologist and photographer, then followed the steps of his own photographic ancestors to the West. In 1977, he cofounded and became chief photographer for "The Rephotographic Survey Project," an ambitious effort to retake—a century later—the epic photographs of the West made in 1870s by the explorers William Henry Jackson and Timothy O'Sullivan. Locating the exact locations—at the same season and time of day—that such iconic images as Jackson's "Mount of the Holy Cross" were made, Klett and his colleagues created a seminal document of physical and cultural change in the West. It was published in 1984 as Second View: The Rephotographic Survey Project.

Now making his home in Tempe, where he is an associate professor at Arizona State University's School of Art, Klett has steadily pursued a goal of reaching "beyond the view" in landscape photography. Between other projects, he has worked on the Desert Citizen *series for the last ten years, compiling hundreds of images. Describing the series as "portraits," he sees his subjects the way the Tohono O'Odham do, as surrogates for humans in the natural world. "What we do to the landscape," he says, "we do to ourselves."*

Stone Bird
Pattiann Rogers

I remember you. You're the one
who lifted your ancient bones
of fossil rock, pulled yourself free
of the strata like a plaster figure
rising from its own mold, became
flesh and feather, took wing,
arrested the sky.

You're the one who, though marble,
floated as beautifully as a white
blossom on the pond all summer,
who, though skeletal and particled
like winter, glimmered as solid as a bird
of cut crystal in the icy trees.

You are redbird—sandstone
wings and agate eyes—at dusk.
You are greybird—polished granite
and pearl eyes—just before dawn,

midnight bird with a reflective
vacancy of heart like a mirror
of pure obsidian.

You're the one who flew down
to that river from the heavens,
as if your form alone were the only
holy message needed. You were alabaster
then in the noonday sun.

Once I saw you rise without rising
from your prison pedestal
in the garden beneath the lime tree.
At that moment your ghost
in its haunting permeated every
regality of the forest with light,
reigned with disdain in thin air
above the mountain, sank in union
with the crosswinds of the sea.

I remember you. You're the one
who entered in through my death
as if it were an open window
and you were the sound of the serenade
being sung outside for me, the words
of which, I know now, are of freedom
cast in stone forever.

MEMORIES of the GROUP THEATRE

An Interview with

DAWN POWELL

By Robert H. Hethmon

Introduction

The following interview, published here for the first time, is not only a delicious read, but a document of no small historical importance, for it's the only known tape-recorded conversation with Dawn Powell.

Powell (1896–1965) was a prolific American author who wrote fifteen novels, ten plays, more than one hundred short stories, thousands of letters, and diaries that span thirty-five years, as well as countless articles and reviews, over five decades of intensive (and usually under-rewarded) labor. Although born in Ohio, Powell spent the last forty-seven years of her life in New York City, mostly in Greenwich Village, and her chronicles of midcentury bohemian life seem both glittering period evocations and absolutely up-to-date.

Out of print and practically forgotten at the time of her death, Powell is now well on her way to becoming a genuinely popular author, with more than a dozen books currently available. Although she gave a number of interviews over the course of her career, whatever she might have said was necessarily distilled by her interlocutor into a few sentences to fit into a newspaper feature. Such pieces are entertaining—Powell always managed to toss off a few funny lines—but they cannot begin to capture the teasing, inventive, and allusive cadences of her conversation, as described by her friends.

How fortunate, then, that a young scholar named Robert H. Hethmon brought along an old Wollensak tape recorder when he visited Dawn Powell in 1965. The recording he made is the only representation we have of Powell's throaty, soft-spoken voice and deadpan delivery. Even in transcription, the Hethmon interview permits us to eavesdrop on one of the century's great storytellers as she recounts her association with the Group Theatre.

Powell knew she was dying when she greeted Hethmon (she had barely three months to live), but she proved a gregarious and funny host. Anybody who has read Powell's diaries will remember that she felt deeply betrayed by the Group Theatre's overly literal, agonizingly earnest production of her first staged play, *Big Night*, a dizzy comedy that closed after only a few performances in early 1933. Yet she was remarkably gracious about her colleagues (most of whom were then still living) and generally treated the whole affair as one more example of human error, something to be laughed off and accepted rather than permitted to poison the spirit.

Tim Page
St. Louis
November 14, 1999

At four o'clock on an August afternoon in 1965, I lugged my tape recorder to the top floor of the apartment building at 95 Christopher Street to call on Dawn Powell—smallish, a bit plump, bright eyed, gracious—to ask about the episode in 1932–1933 when the new Group Theatre was producing her play *Big Night*. She offered me whiskey but would herself drink only ice water: later I learned she was dying of stomach cancer, a fact no word, no inflection revealed.

• • • • • • •

DAWN POWELL: I saw the Group often up at Dover Furnace [*where they had rented a farm for the summer of 1932*]. They were pure, dedicated, almost fey types—more like a splinter religious group than theatrical. They seemed to have little experience of the world. I was startled at their notion of the advertising world of *Big Night* as a gaudy, circus-type set of fancy dressers: in fact, the very image the advertising world—at that early, rather Harvard-y stage—had of *actors*. But they were on the whole an endearing, warm group of people.

ROBERT H. HETHMON: Does that include Stella Adler?

DP: She didn't want to be just a beautiful heroine. She wanted to try out everything. Yes, yes. "Shouldn't she be put in mother parts?" Well, that's what all actresses say, you know, but actually they're pretty sore when they find they're going to play somebody's mother. A couple of years later she *was* the mother in [Clifford] Odets's *Awake and Sing!* And she would wear her gray wig just a little bit off so that people would see she really wasn't old. Then she'd sorta, once in a while, say [*in a heavy Yiddish accent*]: "So you're not happy? So you don't like it at work?" And then she'd look at the audience as if to say, "This is just Stella, really, you know. I'm not really an old lady."

RHH: All these childlike qualities of actors—

DP: Yes, yes.

RHH: It's somehow part of what makes them actors.

DP: I think so, too: "Let's play house."

RHH: Did you know her well?

DP: We were all very chummy. That summer at Dover Furnace, all the writers lived together in a house. I'd go up a few days at a time for rehearsals, and rewrites maybe,

Dawn Powell goes over the script of Big Night with director Cheryl Crawford

and watch. She was the leading lady. They wanted the writers around. Cliff Odets was an actor then, but he was in the writers' house. And sometimes Maxwell Anderson was there to see his wife, who was one of the actresses. Helen Deutsch was publicity agent.

RHH: Jack Lawson was there sometime that summer to work on *Success Story*.

DP: Franchot Tone was going to be the lead in *my* play, and he was very helpful to the Group, because he was more aware of the world than most of them were.

Harold and some of the others were earnest-student types who studied and studied. Or they were sort of semi-debutantes who wanted to be on the stage. Dover Furnace is up near Wingdale. Nearby was a state mental hospital. Some of the patients would wander around, washing windows, doing handy jobs, and everybody got mixed up: which were the people from the Group Threatre and which were the people from the hospital? They all talked the same.

RHH: Passionately? Furiously?

DP: Yes. You could always engage them in talk about their parts. Nobody was quite

IT WAS QUITE a THING, AN ODD LIFE, a kind OF CULT.

sure which was which.

In the kitchen at Dover Furnace—in the old farmhouse—were a couple of Russian guys. They were dishwashers, and *they* were studying Vakhtangov and Stanislavsky, too. It was quite a thing, an odd life, a kind of cult. Cheryl [*Crawford, the director*] was a very practical person, very down-to-earth. Harold was a student. Lee [*Strasberg, the third director*] was the dreamer.

RHH: I suppose it was an accident that had brought you in touch with the Group?

DP: No, it was all part of an extended the-atrical experience. I was hanging around the New Playwrights, Jack Lawson's "people's theater," in 1927 and 1928. I found them a very exciting little outfit. They were writers, Dos Passos, Francis Faragoh, Lawson, Mike Gold, EmJo Basshe. Otto Kahn had given them twenty-five thousand dollars, and with that they did five plays. Kahn and Horace Liveright would appear at their openings in opera capes. I was interested because they were *writers*.

RHH: But their productions were not as good as usual Broadway productions?

DP: No, they were, but they didn't have the money. They were very imaginative. I was so excited and bemused, the way you are by a new thing. At the same time I was working on my first novel, and on my say-so a respectable editor took a group of people down there to Cherry Lane Theatre to take a look. He was new in New York and wanted to be *with it*. I think it was Lawson's *The Internationale*. You know how the excitement of rehearsals and of amateurs can be thrilling. Of course, it's wonderful to see something growing, but then by the time they get it on, it's usually bitched up. So the next day this editor calls me up and says, "Dawn, I will never forgive you for this. I took a very distinguished author of ours and her husband down there to see this

An Interview with Dawn Powell

play you said was so wonderful, and she was so shocked she had a miscarriage." I told this to Jack Lawson, and he said, "Then I think we should charge people for this. Don't have abortions. Just come to see *Internationale* and save yourself of couple of hundred bucks."

RHH: Did they consider doing a play of yours?

DP: They were planning to do my play. There was a great deal of jealousy among those boys, those five male writers, fighting over whose play was to go on next. It was a question whether [they would do] mine or Dos Passos's *Airways, Inc*. I was very fond of Dos, so I said I wanted to be fair and wait until after his play for mine to be done. The reviewers were absolutely furious with all these plays. The boys were furious with each other. And then the money ran out, so the whole thing at the end just petered out.

RHH: So *Big Night* was your second play? How did it get to the Group?

DP: Once I had the script, the day I finished it—I wrote it in ten days; it was called *The Party* then—I took it around, and several producers took an option on it right away. They held it for two years, and that two years' option money was the most I ever made on it. The Theatre Guild was one of those producers, and Harold Clurman, who had been a play reader at the Guild, asked for it in 1932, and my agent, Barrett Clark, arranged for the Guild to release it. The Group—I'm still fond of all of them—paid maybe half of their option: a teaspoonful of option.

RHH: I'm interested that you can look back so philosophically.

DP: Oh, we had a very good time. It was pleasant.

RHH: Some people who have had a play that didn't go so well have found it traumatic.

DP: Yes, I know. They still carry clippings and are still mad at the director.

RHH: Tell me about *Big Night*.

DP: It was in the late twenties. My husband was in advertising, and actually I wrote it out of revenge because he got fired. Everybody called up—the George Cohen office, the William Harris office—and I thought they were friends kidding and would say [*derisively*], "Ah, ah." I couldn't believe it: I had written it so

quickly. I thought it was a light comedy, but evidently the Group thought it was an attack on American manners.

RHH: What did *you* think?

DP: I had written plays in college. I had written the play New Playwrights announced but never did. This first one after that is about a contact man who lives only by the commission from getting the account. He hasn't done any good. He's about to get canned. He's married Myrna, a model from a dress house—that's Stella—and she's a looker and was a big help because the accounts naturally like a handsome girl. But he couldn't stand having fellows paw her. So she had married him: he was taking her away from all that. She didn't work at modeling anymore, but she still has all the clothes from her model job. Then an account comes up, a big dress business from the West: if he can get this account, it will save his life.

And Ed, the husband, finds out that this Jonesy, who's coming to town, is looking for a particular girl at a model house, a girl he used to date: the girl who is now his wife.

"Well," he tells himself, "this is great. It's all made. We'll have him out to the house. He's still crazy about her. Even after a few years he's still looking for her. This is great."

So he tells his wife, and she says, "You mean—you want me to see that old bastard? I wouldn't. Why, I had to fight him all the time. What kind of husband are you?"

"But, look. It'll save our lives. We'll get the account."

"You told me you wanted to get me out of all that, and here you are dragging me in again."

Finally Ed persuades her. Their *whole* existence depends on this. After all, it's the Depression. So they'll have a party for this guy. And he says, "I told him you were crazy to see him."

"You told him—after I threw him out a million times?"

But she's desperate. "What are we going to *do* for a *party*?"

So he says, "I just ran into this fellow on the street I used to know, a nightclub singer. I'll tell him big shots are coming, a big cast, and I'll tell Jonesy about this, and we'll have another couple from the advertising company. We'll have a nice little group."

The wife—Stella—is still upset. She can't stand the idea of seeing this guy again.

RHH: This doesn't sound exactly like a light comedy.

DP: Well, while they're getting ready, a girl, a little cutey from upstairs, comes in and wants to borrow a Spanish shawl: she's

An Interview with Dawn Powell

going to a masquerade and has nothing to wear. She plays up to Ed, who keeps trying to oblige her: "Don't you remember, Myrna? I gave you a Spanish shawl for Christmas." And that makes the wife jealous and mad. "You want me to give *her* my Christmas present?" Then Jonesy arrives.

RHH: J. Edward Bromberg?

DP: What the Group did was this. Joe Bromberg, a wonderful actor, was to be Jonesy. But my Jonesy was a big, lumbering, good-natured, hearty Chicago type. Harold and the Group decided that Joe Bromberg didn't feel comfortable being a Chicago type. It didn't make him happy. He was not happy. He wanted to be a real Jewish type. Well, I didn't know anything about the Jewish dress business. It was not completely Jewish then. It was all different kinds. I didn't know anything about Jewish speech, Jewish expressions. For the Group it was no problem. Just change his name from Jonesy to Schwartzie. That was the first thing that happened.

RHH: Did Franchot play the husband?

DP: By that time Franchot had gone to Hollywood, so they tried different people. They were so dumb. They wanted Russelll Collins, who was a very ugly little man. But in advertising especially the contact men had to be good looking, and the only good-looking guy they had, Lewis Leverett, was not a very good actor, though a good-looking young fellow. That was the second thing.

So there was Jonesy/Schwartzie being extremely Jewish. And the Group had him doing "adjustments" where he learned to love the feel of silk and other textures and,

I THOUGHT
it was a
LIGHT COMEDY,
but evidently
THE GROUP THOUGHT
it was an
ATTACK
on
AMERICAN MANNERS

you know, old European ways.

I got fascinated by all these things they were doing. Here was me—Ohio—with Ohio salesmen, backslapper types that I knew very well. I was fascinated. I wasn't disturbed at all. I just absolutely wondered how they could bring themselves to do all these things.

Bromberg became more and more a *Yiddische papa*.

RHH: What happened?

DP: So they had the party. And everything goes to pot. Clifford Odets was a doorman. The girl comes in, just in the Spanish shawl and nothing else. It had turned out to be the wrong night for the masquerade. And she horns in on the party and sits on everybody's lap and drives the wife more and more crazy. The singer tries to sing, and nobody will listen. And the guy from the office wants to butt in and pretend it's his account. And nobody will let him tell about his army experiences.

Cheryl directed it almost up to the end, and then they thought it was going to pot, so Harold came in and finished it up.

It took them eight months, till January 1933, to make something very strange indeed out of it. It was really fearsome. They made terrifying decisions. Stella would say, "Oh, gee, you know, I feel awfully good today." And they'd say, "But you really don't feel good." So she'd say, "I feel good" and suddenly started crying. Or, else, she'd say, "I feel very sad" and then do a little tap dance. They asked her to do these complicated, neurotic, *mad* things. I was still fascinated by all this, but by the end . . .

RHH: How did it come out?

DP: Everybody gets plastered on speakeasy stuff. The party goes to pot. The third act opens with Ed and Schwartzie together in the fold-up bed— it's only a one-room apartment—and one is upset by a foot sticking out that he thinks is a very repulsive spectacle. He keeps saying, "It isn't human to have a foot like that." They argue about whose foot it is. Stella comes in. The girl from upstairs is still hanging around. And it ends with Stella giving up the whole thing and stalking out—a big Nora thing: "He'll understand it!" But he doesn't: "After all, he was trying to help her. It was as much for her, wasn't it, as for him? For their life together?" So the little girl from upstairs, still in her Spanish shawl, is left—all ready to move in. And it ends when she takes Stella's little dog to the window and gurgles [*a baby voice*]: "Say bye-bye to Mama."

An Interview with Dawn Powell

RHH: How did you feel when it was all over?

DP: Well, to my astonishment, people exploded with such indignation. I thought a lot of the play was very funny, but everybody took it that I really didn't know I was being noncomformist. Their point of view was utterly, completely American: the wife *should* have helped her husband by being nice to the boss. That was the beginning of that kind of thing—all wives are supposed to be nice to the boss so the guy can get ahead.

RHH: *Oil for the Lamps of China?*

DP: Yes, yes. People were standing in the aisles. And a woman was crying: "I can't stand it. Who is this Dawn Powell that she makes Stella Adler be such a terrible woman to her husband? And this is so anti-Semitic, making Schwartzie such an awful man." But I hadn't anti-Semitized it: the Semites had. I thought the audience would be saying what I would have said, that the play was a rather feeble light comedy, but everybody was indignant. They carried on so.

RHH: They missed the satire of advertising?

DP: Yes. They thought the play

Stella Adler and Joe Bromberg in a scene from Powell's 1933 production of Big Night.

was an insult to the American Way. And that's when I realized I didn't myself know what was the American Way.

RHH: Did the press like it?

DP: Well, I went back to my house. Faragoh and Jack Lawson and my husband and a lot of other people came in, and they said, "The papers haven't come yet." I went to bed. It was all over, and I was glad of it. But finally I woke up: "What's the matter? It's four o'clock. The papers are always out by this time." And my husband said, "My dear, I don't want you to see them." Well, of course, I *knew* they weren't good. I could tell from the audience. People at the house were shaking their heads and saying—about my feeble little, you know—"Oh, this is brutal! Ohhh! Ohhh!"

Then I saw the reviews. Well, I was delighted with them. They said, "This is so powerful—this powerful attack on advertising. Miss Powell doesn't know what a script she has. It's too strong for the theater. Her touch is too powerful." And I thought, My goodness, if I can pink that old elephant hide, I've got it! I was so encouraged that that very day I started a new play.

RHH: Do you think the Group actors somehow converted your play into . . .

DP: Yes, into meaningfulness. Everything was made meaningful.

RHH: Portentous?

DP: They made it portentous, when it could have been played lightly. But who knows? As a light little thing, it could have been a flop just the same.

RHH: The Group never produced a really witty play.

DP: They said [*pompously*]: "Wit is a good thing! Sometimes wit is a very good thing to have!" I wasn't impressed with what they

WITH 'BIG NIGHT' I DROVE THEM *into the* WOODS.

did with actors' emotions. Good actors always feel their part anyway. They were so pretentious about getting into it and pacing up and down. They were always studying Vakhtangov!

When Stella was in Paris some years later, she met Stanislavsky and discussed everything with him. And he said, "You've done everything wrong. That isn't what I said at all. You've misunderstood my Method completely."

RHH: Did the play go pretty far in rehearsal at Dover Furnace?

DP: They were there all summer. The play really went eight months in rehearsal—and lasted seven days on Broadway.

RHH: But that summer and fall they were also working on Lawson's *Success Story*.

DP: The Lawsons had a house out at the shore, and we had a place right next to it. So Jack and I would go out there straight from our workout with the Group. And at the time he was making fun of the comrades and the Communist touches. The Group was a pretty Red outfit. And he was very jolly about that. But I haven't caught him laughing since then. We ended our friendship because I'm such a fascist. He can't stand anybody anymore who isn't a Communist. That was too bad. He was so good. *Processional* was such a wonderful play. And *Roger Bloomer*. And I was crazy about *Loudspeaker*. It was so funny. Leonard Sillman [*later a well-known Broadway producer*] was a butler. They had this roller-coaster set. The governor's wife was halfway up in a ticket booth with a mud pack on her face. And the butler made his entrance down a chute on roller skates. There was a girl in a bathing suit—Miss New Lots. Jack was very good, but then he disowned all those things and got into pure polemics.

RHH: In the winter—before the summer in Dover Furnace—the Group did an agit-prop play by the Siftons called *1931* and Maxwell Anderson's *Night over Taos*.

DP: Oh, yes. But after that I broke them up. With *Big Night* I drove them into the woods. They were dismantled, weren't they?

RHH: They couldn't do anything then until summer.

DP: Everybody was broke. They finally got a house somewhere. Everybody would bring in five cents, and they would have a loaf of bread. If somebody had a job, he would feed everybody. They were an absolutely loyal, dedicated outfit. Cheryl after this took on more and more of the financial responsibility. Harold was killing himself over Stella. You know. Love. L'amour. Lee just stood in the background as a sort of teacher. And afterwards I didn't see much of them.

RHH: Did you get out of theater?

DP: No, I think *Big Night* would have flopped even if it had been done as a light comedy—as I thought it should have been. It would have flopped even more so. This way I saw I could do something. My next play, *Jig Saw*, which I started as a really meaningful play, a selfish-mother play, I immediately began to make as a French farce. I wrote it in terms of "Oh, papa! Oh, here comes Adèle, the French maid!" Doors opening and shutting all the time. No one ever suspected I intended any meaning at all. The Theatre Guild took it, the very day I finished it. And everybody at the Guild was going over to Europe that summer [1934]—a cruise on the English waterways, or maybe it was the fjords—and they wanted to get everything out of the way. I never had to rewrite a line. They just wanted a sixth play to fulfill their subscription so they could get on the boat. Even so, some people found that what actually came out as a light, foolish little thing was in their opinion sharp satire. I never could find it. It's my defect. What I think is realism, everybody else calls "a savage attack."

Later I wrote some more plays that

Dawn Powell at the time of the interview, summer 1965, in her Christopher Street apartment. Photo by Carol Warstler.

An Interview with Dawn Powell

always had options, until I got so tired of options. They don't give you time to do anything else, and I wanted to write novels, too. Somebody is calling up all the time—somebody's office boy who has decided he is a producer. And you have to see them all just in case it might be another Jed Harris. So I had to stop myself. And I enjoyed writing dialogue. I got praise: you'd get more out of just a little bit of playwriting than out of a lifetime of any other kind of writing.

RHH: Was Cheryl's direction so bad they were justified in taking her off your play?

DP: I think she got herself off of it. It was just three or four days before opening. I think maybe she was just worn out. They all agreed. They were very happy to agree with each other. I wouldn't have known. It was all the same to me.

RHH: They had a tendency to read a kind of significance into certain plays, which . . .

DP: It's always better to let it seep through, to let people find out without knowing they are learning. Instead of shaking your fist.

RHH: Did they discuss with you what your play meant?

DP: Oh, yeah. All the time. And I am not anybody who wants to . . . I mean I want to do it, write it, and then let the audience find itself in it. I loathe discussion groups, and I don't want actors prowling around undressed in my subconscious. I think the Groupers really would have liked to have a footnote to everything said on the stage. In those days people wore these funny, formal clothes to the theater. They brought—call it imagination—to the theater, and in many cases they took away . . . magic.

> *It's my* **DEFECT,** *what I think is* **REALISM,** **EVERYBODY ELSE** *calls* **"A SAVAGE ATTACK."**

RHH: Did *any* of the Group's productions have this magic?

DP: They did well with Irwin Shaw. *The Gentle People* was good, but again, that was Franchot Tone. A lot of naturally good actors can stand hearing about the Method, just as a lot of beautiful women can stand some bad makeup and still come out beautiful. Franchot was an intelligent kind of smooth actor, not a great actor, but he was . . . he had intelligence. Sandy Meisner was a smart boy. Tony Kraber was good. Joe Bromberg was a naturally good actor. Not very many highly intelligent people were there. I think they loved casting against type, making somebody good who was not made for the part. That was part of showing they were *actors*.

RHH: Did you find them particularly political the summer of 1932?

DP: They were beginning to be. Definitely bent that way, definitely Reddish. Of course, they were crazy about what was going on in Russia, the Russian theater, the Russian Revolution, the Russian . . . everything. They were completely gone. I was myself. Most young people were. I think some of them were Communists, and anxious to angle everything that way. It got more so after I was gone, after my gentle

> I DON'T *want* ACTORS PROWLING *around* UNDRESSED *in my* SUBCON-SCIOUS.

Ohio Methodist-Baptist-Lutheran influence was gone. They were very pleasant, very romantic.

I went out to Hollywood to visit. I was there for a month in September 1936 at the Chateau Elysée, and Joe Bromberg said, "I'll take you to a little Group hideout." And we went to this house where they were having a Group conclave. It was a vacant house somebody had managed to get the money to rent, and they were having classes and continuing with the Group

Method. We peeked through the door, and I saw several people, my old buddies, that I recognized. And Bromberg and I began getting convulsions because the head of the class, one of the members, was saying: "No, no, not at all. This dinner is a Thanksgiving dinner. We're having turkey, and you're making a face as if we are having red wine, but it's white wine. Begin all over again. No, no. You still are having red wine . . . . That's it. That's it. That's the white wine no . . . . You've got it." So we tiptoed around to where another scene was going on, and it was the same. "No, no, you have just told her you love her, but you aren't sure whether you really do or not. You're thinking it over. Now, you said 'I love you' as if it was true. But you aren't sure in your own heart." Oh, they went through terrific ordeals. Even though they were looking for jobs out there, they wanted to practice to keep up their Method. They wanted to keep it up. They were all pretty broke. A desperate winter for most of them, except Bromberg, who was doing all right. He was amused by Hollywood and amused by the Group. He was really first rate as an actor.

RHH: So you saw some of the Group people over the years?

DP: Yes. Some were sort of lost. They had wanted to see if they had something. Often they found out they didn't. But I don't think they knew it. And I don't think they got a lot out of it. A man I've seen off and on, Art Smith, I ran into him a few years ago. He's a little, tiny fellow, and he had an enormous wolfhound. My husband and I about six years ago were staying in some hotel in Gramercy Park, the Irving, and there was Art and this big dog and an even bigger wife. "Dawn! How good to see you! Could you lend me five bucks?" Nobody lived at that hotel unless you were pretty broke anyway, but I raised it for him. And he said, "We'll get it for you. My wife has got a job." And the wife said [*shouting*], "You're not borrowing money again, are you?" And he said, "Honey, it's Saturday. Where are we going to get it?" Well, he was very funny.

Then I moved away from there. About a year or so later he called up one day and said, "Dawn, I've been worried about you. I haven't seen you for a long time. How are things going?" And I said, "Fine. Everything's grand. I finished a book." Whatever you say in those circumstances. "And how are *you*?" He said, "Great. We've been having a wonderful time lately. None of these hard-luck stories. Can you loan me five dollars?" I said, "Sure." They had a one-room apartment with two cats and this big dog. And they stayed in bed all the time, so

they were always in pretty poor shape. He didn't have any top on his pajamas, and she just had a bra on, they were always reading the *Journal-American*. And he had a big gallon of red wine, which he would drink right out of: "Do you want some of this here? We don't have any cups here." And the wife's mother also lived there in an apartment: the hotel clerks explained that the mother was very rich, but gaga, so they had her parked there so they could tap her from time to time. And she had an attendant, a colored maid, who was drunk all the time, and she'd come down and say, "Art, let me have some of that stuff, will you?" So he'd say, "Here you are. Have a snort there, Hettie." So it was a fine life. He would do *Uncle Vanya* or something off-Broadway, but he said it was better to be on unemployment because of the low off-Broadway scale. He must be around somewhere. You might case all the small, dingy hotels around Madison Square.

RHH: Was your husband ever in the theater?

DP: No, as a very young man, he had been a drama critic on a Pittsburgh paper. He had gone to the theater since he was a child. He saw every play that was on the road from about 1906 and carefully wrote down his opinions of it. But when he got to New York, he went into advertising. And I think he always regretted it. Like all advertising men: "I was happy when I was on a newspaper." He died about three or four years ago, of cancer. I still don't know what to do with all these twelve-year-old-boy's impressions of Clyde Fitch.

RHH: A last word on the Group?

DP: I'm afraid I've said bad things about it. Will you cut all that out? What they were doing, it seemed to me, was the natural thing for anybody to do. Like a person doesn't need all those fancy words in psychoanalysis to straighten themselves out. A real actor could find it himself. I doubt if it affected the genuine actors at all. Well, they made a lot of people very happy, like a religion. Evidently it saved a lot of people somehow. They seemed to find something in it.

. . . .

On the day of this interview, Dawn Powell wrote in her diary: "Must go to hospital fast for transfusions. Also intestinal something." On November 8, 1965, she entered St. Luke's Hospital for the last time. She died on Sunday, November 14. Ultimately her remains were buried in the city cemetery on Hart Island in a mass grave. In my memory she lingers as a truly gallant lady. ◼

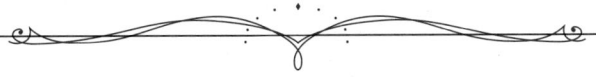

PROFILES™

Visiting Mr. Sanford

NEIL GORDON

Neil Gordon profiles John Sanford, a singular Jewish-American writer who dared to stand up to Senator McCarthy.

I. There is a story my mother tells about a young man who journeys to the farthest Himalayas in search of a famous guru. For months he travels, braving hardship and peril, storm and snow, surmounting all odds, until one day he arrives at the guru's hermitage. Gasping for breath, he says, "Master, I have traveled around the world to ask you for the answer." The guru, sitting in the lotus position, gazes at him for a long time before finally, breaking years of silence, he asks—for some reason, this part is always told in a Yiddish accent—

"Nu, vot is the question?"

A brilliant sun fell through perfectly dry air the morning I set out from Los Angeles to visit John Sanford, the kind of sun and the kind of air that make you remember that much of California is coastal chaparral. The night before, I had flown, at my own expense, from New York; that night I would fly back. I had come to spend an hour with a ninety-four-year-old writer of whom nearly no one in the entire country has heard, and as I went north along the coast on this January morning, as I had been doing for months, I kept rehearsing and rejecting the questions I had come to ask.

Close to Santa Barbara, the highway passes a seemingly endless sea of opulent suburbs. The exit ramp to the neighborhood I was trying to find left me climbing shaded streets of gated properties, each advertising an armed private security company on a lawn placard. Sanford's house, with no visible number on the street, was difficult to identify. When I at last pulled up a driveway—at random, really—I recognized from his autobiography the Jaguar in the garage, one of a series given him by his wife, a successful screenwriter, throughout their fifty years of marriage.

Now, like the sixties searcher from my mother's story, I had come to journey's end. I was perfectly on time, a couple minutes before ten. The January morning was glorious: the Santa Ynez Mountains behind me, the Pacific Ocean before. The house in its pleasant yard sat in cool, shaded silence under the enormity of the California sky, showing no sign of life.

And still, I was not sure what the question was.

2.

A year earlier, working on my own second novel in New York, I had first encountered John Sanford in Griffin Fariello's oral history of the Hollywood blacklist, *Red Scare*.

> **In '52, a guy from the State Department came around and wanted our passports back. I told him to fuck himself. I says, "Nothing doing. They belong to me." He said, "Well, that's true that the piece of cardboard belongs to you. But don't ever try to use it, because we'll stop you." . . .**
>
> **You have no idea what it is to be in a jail that's three thousand miles wide. You could walk your ass off, but you were still in jail.**

John Sanford. I knew him also from the catalogs of Black Sparrow Press, that publisher of the virtual pléiade of American avant-garde writing from Mina Loy to Charles Bukowski, about which I had written several articles. Now, I wrote away for five of the eight titles they had in print. The day they arrived, boxed and tied in brown paper and string, was the last I saw of my own work for several months to come.

The five titles, I saw, made up a single work, fifteen hundred pages long. It was subtitled *Scenes from the Life of an American Jew,* and the whole composed the autobiography of an American writer who between 1935 and the present had published some twenty-two books, the last in 1996. A New Yorker born and bred, he had spent his adult life entirely in California; like John Fante and Bukowski, he was a Depression veteran and a Los Angeleno. As such, he fit Black Sparrow's profile perfectly. And though I felt some surprise that I had never heard of such a Jewish and leftist writer—no doubt, when I looked, I'd find an article by Alfred Kazin or Irving Howe about him—I still felt on fairly steady ground.

But what I read, when I began to read, didn't fit any of the categories I had prepared for it. And that was where the questions began.

3.

If *Scenes from the Life of an American Jew* begins in familiar territory, that familiarity is only glancing. In fact, I quickly realized as I read, a gulf as big as the whole country separates this writer from, say Henry Roth, or Bernard Malamud, or other chroniclers of Jewish immigrant life in New York. For one thing, the five volumes of Sanford's autobiography are composed entirely of short, cinematic scenes from the author's life, each appearing with the allure of a few short feet of long-lost film. And still, that was not all that was unique about this writing.

From the first word, I saw, the author is interested not in the autobiographical project of documenting his past, but rather in the more artistically challenging one of dramatizing its unknowability.

In scene 1 the author's father, arriving in New York from Lithuania in 1883, is five years old: "If he remembered his days and nights in steerage, he never spoke of the ways in which they were spent; he never made mention of the sights he'd seen, the sky's colors, the spray-savor, the games and cries of other children, and you never knew the name and size of the ship." *You*, I saw, was the author: this was an autobiography in the second person singular, as if the author addressed himself. Scene 2 described "you's" mother, born in 1881 in the Lower East Side of New York—or rather, described the impossibility of describing her: "Somewhere a doorway she entered, a shop, a school; she was in being once on certain streets, in certain rooms and minds; but no record remains of her presence, and few who knew her are now alive." The author is not born until scene 9, when the vast, firmly established Jewish Lithuanian family born of two sets of transplanted grandparents is well settled in their homes in Mount Morris, in then-Jewish Harlem, and their thriving businesses—real estate, law practices—downtown, have been described. Then, the day of his birth—May 31, 1904—is captured in another cinematic exposition of its disappearance: "They're all dead now, those who may have been there for the event, and lost with them the look of the place, the disposition of the furniture, the pattern of the paper on

> *As I read the five volumes, one after the other, I understood that there was nothing familiar about this territory. This was unlike anything I had ever read in my life.*

the wall. . . . You try to force your memory, but long before it reaches your beginning, it ends in swirling sleeves of steam." Strange stuff, but oddly seductive. The second-person-singular address worked, as in the few other books I've seen it used well: Jay McInerney's good second book, Stewart O'Nan's wonderful last one. It drew me directly into that comfortable world of established Jews in New York—early immigrants who achieved quick success in the professions and settled uptown even while new immigrants struggled on the Lower East Side—at the turn of the century, when the relations and mythologies of the shtetl flourished in the opulence and safety of the new land. But all sense of familiarity fled the moment I completed scene 13, "Summer at Tannersville" (a town in the Catskill Mountains' Borscht Belt) and the action shifted to . . .

Roanoke Island, North Carolina, in 1587, when the first white baby in America was born, Virginia Dare, of whom it is known only that she was dead by 1591. When her grandfather, John White, returned to America after a victualing trip home to England—a return trip over the Atlantic that took nearly four years—the landing party of 116 people was gone.

There were voices on the sand and in the air, but they spoke no tongue that White could understand. There were clouds of heron crying as if an army of men had shouted together; there were parrots, falcons, and merlinbaws; there were clam-birds, there were wrens in the cattail, there were plover and willet and clapper-rail—but their cries made no sense in English ears, and the search, begun at that right-hand gatepost, ended there.

What was this? A different kind of "scene," one in which the author salvaged the trace of unknowable moments not from his own past, or his family's, but that of his country. Segments like this, titled "The Color of the Air," are interspersed throughout the progress of this strange autobiography, describing historical figures from the history of the Americas, from Francisco de Coronado ("In the year of the incarnation of the Lord 1540, Francisco de Coronado, with 300 horse, marched northward from Culiacan to seek the Seven Cities of Cibola that had been voiced for by Fran Marcos de Niza") to John Wilkes Booth ("The derringer weighed half a pound. The ball weighed half an ounce"), and a monologue in the voice of Crazy Horse that, I saw, opened the full possibilities of this form:

Beside the Little Big Horn, much fine killing was done that day, wherefore truly had Curly spoken when he called it a good day for dying: when whites died, it was always a good day. But what we did not know then, savoring their blood and wearing their hair, was that we too were now dead, not some of us but all, those of us still under horses in the high grass and those singing in stolen hats and the tops we cut from the soldiers' boots—all.

It was a good day to die, Curly said, and thereafter we never lived again.

It was the end of living for us, that victory in the hills where the Tongue River rose, and the Rosebud ran.

As I read the five volumes, one after the other, I understood that there was nothing familiar about this territory. This was unlike anything I had ever read in my life.

It was, in fact, unlike anything anyone else had ever written.

Compare it, for example, to Sanford's closest mainstream Jewish contemporary, Henry Roth, a writer whose first, innovative novel of Jewish life in New York was published in the thirties at the same time as Sanford's first novel, and who wrote four volumes of autobiography in the 1980s, just when Sanford was writing his.

Heavily subject to the literary and political influences swirling around New York in the thirties, the two writers share many similarities, despite Roth's childhood poverty and the comparative comfort of Sanford's earlier-established family. But there is a more fundamental, and fundamentally telling, difference between the two. For despite the self-conscious surface experimentalism, fundamental to Roth's form of autobiography is his neurotic insistence on the narcissistic imperative—"who am I?"—whereas Sanford, with his surprising second-person-singular address and his photographic technique, is asking a question philosophically more complex, one that derives more from the modernism in which Rimbaud wrote "I is an other" than from the therapeutic Freudian tradition of Roth.

Sanford's autobiography, subversive in style and substance, courageous in its often nearly heartless honesty, deeply beautiful in its clean, direct prose, asks not who, but *what* is I—not just a personal question, but also a profound existential one. What is the I, always changing, that we carry through time? What remains of "I" when all that defined it has changed, or died? How much of "I" is self-constituted, and how much the construction of history, of politics, of religion, of family, of love? Nor are these questions posed self-consciously or intellectually, but always with the highest conception of art, of the delicate sublimation of message to the imperatives of medium.

There's pathos attached, a pathos born of the urgency of Sanford's effort to capture the materiality of his long experience of time, and so the text is inhabited by a constant sense of loss. This sounds familiar, but it's not: while Sanford tends less toward Roth than toward Proust or Albert Cohen, Jewish chroniclers of transcendent experience of a lost world, he's also after something more: not only to capture—or, to use Sanford's term, salvage the materiality of time, but also to subvert the concept of identity.

For as soon as he turns to Virginia Dare, or Lincoln's assassin, or Crazy Horse, he ups the ante beyond anything even dreamed of by Roth. The "Color of the Air" segments, again and again, recast his personal identity within the history of exploitation, violence, racism, Red-baiting, and overt favoring of the rich: traditions, Sanford insists, as American—to extend H. Rap Brown's famous quote—as cherry pie, which the author uses to dwarf the importance of his own subjectivity while exploring how that subjectivity is shaped by the brute injustice of human life.

The result is a huge, utterly original achievement, a questioning of the nature of the human through the lens of an expansive, liberal Judaism on the level of Yehoshua; an invocation of time and lost place equal to Proust's, a testament to love, filial and matrimonial, comparable to Mann's.

How is it then that the lesser work, Roth's, was rediscovered by Irving Howe and, in a single *New York Times Book Review* article, lifted to the pinnacle of literary fame, while Sanford's autobiography went nearly entirely unnoticed? That, I felt sure, was the most urgent question.

4.

The children and grandchildren of John Sanford's generation are everywhere in America, the widespread, varied, and entirely vested community of American Jews who occupy just about every social level in the country, from taxi driver to Secretary of State. Frequently—in fact, most often—their primary allegiances lie outside their community: their cultural, religious, or tribal Judaism is a secondary or even tertiary loyalty in their lives. And yet they share an enormous homogeneity of cultural background—the Americanized version of an Ashkanazic heritage, that civilization that developed between the fifteenth-century expulsion of the Jews from Spain and the Holocaust.

Sanford's father took part in the mass-migration from Lithuanian cities and shtetls to escape both pogrom and conscription, at thirteen, straight out of heder, into the czarist army—my own grandparents left for South Africa in the same migration, which continued unabated until 1939. His father came to America young, early enough to earn a law degree at Fordham University when Fordham was housed in the Woolworth Building. Sanford himself was born Julian Shapiro in 1904, a first-generation American in a thriving, widespread family.

Nothing could be more recognizable to an American Jew than this background, and across this country there are professionals of every possible stripe who recognize their own fathers and grandfathers in that child from Mount Morris, standing before the Jewish American dream that led, for his peers, to the pinnacles of prestige, security, and comfort. But there is not another soul in the history of America who lived quite the life that Sanford has.

For although he would take his own law degree at Fordham, instead of adding his name to the sign on his father's glass-windowed door at Beekman Court he would ride freight trains across America and steamers to Europe, ultimately fleeing Spain on the eve of the Civil War. And although his father would be his life's central influence, it would be his strange uncle Dave, a merchant sea-

> *There is not another soul in the history of America who lived quite the life that Sanford has.*

man whose greatest experience was receiving a letter from Socialist Party leader Eugene Debs during his imprisonment for violating the Espionage Act, who would turn him into a life-long Communist. His leftist literary ambition would be solidified by reading William Carlos Williams's *In the American Grain,* and these ambitions would be challenged by Senator Joseph McCarthy, who subjected him to ten years of internal exile.

Above all, nothing predicted that he would be convinced by the example of his childhood friend from Mount Morris, Natchie Weinstein, to abandon the law and become a novelist, which he did, publishing his first novel, *The Waterwheel,* just after Natchie, as Nathanael West, published *Miss Lonelyhearts,* his second.

Or that under the name John Sanford he would, over the rest of the century, write and publish an oeuvre of American fiction unlike any other that ever has or ever will be written. As I moved beyond the autobiography and hunted down Sanford's work in rare-book libraries and used-book stores, I found a number of early novels born of the same modernist revolution as were those of Nathanael West, although they quickly diverged, tending toward the "radical" novels of James T. Farrell and John Dos Passos with which they are associated today. Next came the unique volumes of American "historical commentary"—vignettes scrupulously dramatizing moments of injustice and heroism in American history—which are an entirely unique literary form (although Eduardo Galeano's writings today bear an enormous sympathy). Then the five-volume autobiography, which has been followed by a stream of volumes about his wife, virtually the sole subject about which Sanford writes anymore.

But it is far more by its reception than its actual content that John Sanford's work is most often known—to the very, very few, that is, who know of it at all. For as quickly as it could be written, it slipped beneath the surface of American literary attention like a perfect Atlantis falling into the depths. It has never been lost: a publisher was found for all of Sanford's works (a single title was self-published, and later acquired by Black Sparrow Press); PEN West Coast has honored him; the *Los Angeles Times* recently awarded him the Robert Kirsch Award, a lifetime-achievement honor; an impressive market exists for his first editions; and a small, dedicated audience has come to follow him—even now a new book is waiting to be published by Capra, the highly respected West Coast small press. But his work has never fully come into the light, existing in a netherworld of those who fail to find a place in the mainstream.

Happiness, wrote Tolstoy, follows few rules, but the failure to be happy, many. All successful writers are alike, for fame covers all differences, but each unsuccessful writer is so in his own way. Yet neither Sanford's success nor his failure is like that of anyone else, so much so that it is difficult to say, exactly, which is which.

So, rather than illustrating the nature of literary success and failure, John Sanford's unique life and work puts into question exactly what success and failure, in literary matters, have come to mean.

Perhaps, I thought, that was what I needed to ask.

5.

Nothing, points out Russell Banks, is of use to a writer as much as luck: luck to make the right contacts, luck to get the right kind of publicity, luck to find the right audience. Legion are the writers who have been kept from audiences by hard luck: look at West himself, whose *Miss Lonelyhearts* was published to rave reviews by a bankrupt publisher who could not put the book into stores. And yet, as I learned about John Sanford, I saw that since his early association with West, he seems to have been guided only by the best fortune.

It's the story everybody likes to hear, an adjunct to the backstage drama of the understudy's chance at the lead role. The young Jewish writers of the thirties who were snapped up by the studio system were legion: I have met them in their capacious homes with Chagalls on the walls and sailboats in the marina and an oeuvre of horror films and B Westerns, to their shame, behind them. By the time Sanford's call came, just after the publication of his second novel, *The Old Man's Place,* he had set the stage for it to perfection: despite his father's illness, despite his family fortune having been lost in the Depression, and despite possessing a perfectly serviceable law degree, he had for years been living on change from his father's pocket, devoting himself entirely to reading and writing. Paramount's call was the stuff writers' dreams are made of: 350 1936 dollars per week for six months and options totaling two hundred thousand dollars. It is the first act of a morality play everyone loves to see again and again, for it holds not only the winning jackpot to close the act, but the sure promise of retribution. By act II, the young hero is sure to sell out, and we will have the pleasure of seeing him, like so many others, leave talent behind for money. Should that fail, well, there is the ever-present threat of alcoholism, and then there is the House Un-American Activities Committee lurking in act III. One way or another that original drama is sure to end up with our hero either a fink or a failure.

Except—not here.

Summoned to Hollywood by Paramount, not only did Sanford refuse to make the slightest creative compromise for screen work, but indeed directed himself as surely toward unemployment on the West Coast as he had on the East, characteristically alienating those who employed him, predictably failing to connect with the powerful (despite brief early friendships with Joan Crawford and Jean Muir), befriending the marginal, the homosexual, the leftist. Never did he bend his talent to an assignment, but steadily worked toward being fired at every opportunity, and Sanford was fired by the best of them. Lest I give the wrong impression, it should be made clear that rarely, by his own accounting, did he ever conduct his professional writing life with anything but the most singular lack of grace: touchy, proud, irritable, and utterly hostile to editing, Sanford in Hollywood alienated every possible patron as quickly as when, years before in New York, he had withdrawn a short story from the first issue of William Carlos Williams's celebrated magazine, *Contact*—included work by Williams, West, e.e. cummings, Zukofsky—after Dr. Williams suggested the sexually suggestive title be changed.

And here's where the story leaves the established track we all love to follow. For within months of his arrival in Hollywood, the two Freudian axes of Sanford's life, love and work, met permanently in the form of Margueritte Roberts, the highly respected career screenwriter at MGM (she scripted, among many other films, *Dragon Seed,* with Katharine Hepburn, *Sea of Grass,* with Spencer Tracy and Hepburn, *Ivanhoe,* with Elizabeth Taylor and Robert Taylor, and *Ziegfeld Girl,* with James Stewart and Lana Turner). Roberts would become Sanford's wife, and her massive earnings as a contract writer for MGM made any income derived from his own writing superfluous.

Now the morality play is over, and no longer does this story have the audience it opened to. It is a story of how a Lithuanian Jew from New York and a third-generation American from Clark, Nebraska, lived and worked, the one writing popular pictures, the other obscure novels, in the quiet and benign comfort of Southern California in the days before the freeways.

They ran horses, dined at Musso and Frank, took care of their parents, had friends. Roberts's quote increased with each new contract; Sanford wrote and, although he struggled, published with all the biggest houses of his day: Boni, Knopf, Hitchcock.

And so would have gone Sanford's hapless journey toward happiness, were there not at the center of it two tragedies.

First was HUAC. Sanford, whose conscience had grown with his fortunes, had by the mid-forties joined the Communist Party, and he and Roberts—both of whom pleaded the Fifth before HUAC—would experience nearly a decade on the blacklist, years in which love and work would be put to the test. And the second tragedy is the story of another, perhaps related, blacklisting: this one not by Hollywood because of politics, but by publishers because of art.

Among the most vivid pictures John Sanford paints is that of the complex of influences that drew many thinking people, particularly Jews, into the party in the late thirties. There were the contemporary threats of the rise of fascism abroad and of opposition to injustice at home. From volume three of his autobiogrphy: "Father Coughlin, the K-K-K, support for the worker, the Negro, Spain." There was the deep American heritage of radicalism, personified by John Brown. For Sanford, there was also the ever-present figure of his uncle Dave. And there was the gathering war—not just that against fascism, but the more ominous one that was becoming increasingly evident as the decade drew to its end: the mounting war against the Jews of Europe, which no one—no one in the world—was moving to oppose.

And yet nowhere is better painted the contradiction between the high idealism of the aims and the absolute vileness of the methods of Hollywood Communists: the restrictions on relationships and expression, the backbiting, the cowardliness, and the money hunger, the cheating. For Sanford, the blacklisting that McCarthy would render legal started long before, and it was trifold. First was the blacklisting by the party itself, in the face of whose literary disapproval Sanford found himself writing. Then was the blacklist of such organs as the Dies Committee, who accused Sanford of the bizarre crime of being a "Premature Anti-fascist," and so denied him a commission on Frank Capra and William Wyler's war-propaganda work, not to mention the chance to serve in the army. But none of these were more than distant thunder compared to the storm clouds that gathered over American Communists after the war.

How bad, precisely, the blow of a HUAC subpoena was is hard to imagine today. The Sanfords' suffering, in particular, tends to be underestimated. MGM's generous—in context—decision to pay out Margueritte Roberts's contract relieved them of any of the dire financial hardship that other unfriendly witnesses faced, and their immediate response to the blacklist, prior to the confiscation of their passports, was to order an MG for delivery in London and leave on a grand tour.

But money relieved only a part of the suffering inflicted by the Congressional Red hunt, for if the rejection of a writer by the public is harsh, rejection by his peers is virtually unbearable. From the moment they were placed on the blacklist, the Sanfords found themselves isolated from their professional, social, and literary communities: unable to work, without passports, and, worse, out of favor within the Communist networks that one might have expected to support them. What followed were ten years of internal exile; ten years of rejection by family and friends, within and without the Party; ten years of a punishment as bad as can be imposed on a writer, for until the lifting of the blacklist in 1960, Margueritte Roberts was largely unable to work and John Sanford, in empathy and out of guilt, refused also to do so.

The blacklist, however, ultimately failed to silence either of them. Margueritte Roberts wrote some of her most successful films in the sixties—including *True Grit* for John Wayne—and Sanford, too, returned to work.

In fact, as I looked closer into Sanford's story, I saw that McCarthy was the least of the enemies he faced.

To alienate both the most powerful critical voice in the country as well as one of its most promising literary talents—all in a single publishing season—is a rare accomplishment in any age. Sanford, pulling his story from *Contact* and calling West, in public, a "sheeny in Brooks clothing," carried it off with the same efficiency with which he would, in the long writing career to follow, argue with nearly every editor and publisher he had. He would neither be edited nor edit himself, refusing to change either politics or prose to suit either political realities or aesthetic demands, and he endured rejection after rejection for each book he published, going as far as to publish one himself. A 1945 exchange with John Woodburn, editor at Harcourt Brace, which Sanford recreated in his autobiography, tells all:

> **He said, "I'm authorized to say we'll take the book if you get rid of the politics." "By whom?" "The editor-in-chief." "Tell him I'll be thinking of him next time I wipe my ass."**

Yet publish he would, and if it was often to reviews of the kind that can stop writing careers in their tracks, there was also support from unexpected sources. Of his second novel John Chamberlain wrote in the preeminently influential daily *New York Times* review: "[Sanford] is to the novel what the school of Thomas Benton or Grant Wood is to painting—a 'nativist' who takes a purely aesthetic delight in the salt and savor, even in the occasional flaring brutality, of the American Character. His *The Old Man's Place* is a first attempt to catch this character on the wing, and his ambition is to make his next novel as American as Brady's pictures." And the same John Woodburn who later, at Harcourt Brace, would have the unenviable task of delivering his employer's political censorship, originally championed him with this editorial note: "I can give Harcourt an author who will replace Dos Passos at his best. We launched Red Lewis, and we published Dos and Djuna Barnes and Katherine Anne Porter, and they reappear, these special ones, each in his Generation—and here, by God, is Sanford...."

The single novel that Sanford was unable to sell and had to self-publish was *A Man Without Shoes*, in 1951. Dalton Trumbo, in exile in Mexico after being jailed for his Hollywood Ten defiance of HUAC, wrote to Sanford:

> I think I have some idea of what you went through with it. I was in jail ten months and missed parole once and finally got out upon the expiration of the term. You must've been in jail with this for five years, and Paul tells me you missed parole thirty-four times, and finally had to buy your way out.
>
> What a disgrace, what a vomitous comment on American publishers, what a terrifying thing to all writers that you had to publish it yourself.... In any event, for this book and for my money, you can piss on any author who has been published in this country in the last five years... and if, in the process, you spatter your boots a little, send them to me and I'll clean them for you.

True, voices like Trumbo's championed Sanford even in the sea of McCarthyite disapproval. But there were also miserable reviews, reviews of a mean-spiritedness few American critics would display today. "An Unpleasant Egoist" headed a *Times* review; a *Miami Herald* reviewer wrote of *The Waterwheel*, "This is a first novel. It should be the last.... There is little action, the narrative dealing with the indecent and horrible sentiments and certain sexual experiences of our scavenger hero. While we are no friend of censorship, yet the publication of such bilge as this will call for a stop." As for *The Nation*, of *The Old Man's Place*, they wrote, more cryptically than critically, "Irresponsible books like this warn the revolutionary writers to be morally and stylistically more careful than ever."

Combined with Sanford's insistence on speaking his mind, often alienating even his supporters, the effect was dire. Without influential critical help, without mainstream positive reviews, and above all without the steady support of a publisher willing to create a new

"What a disgrace, what a vomitous comment on American publishers"

audience, Sanford's writing slipped steadily beneath the surface of public attention.

If the question is How did this brilliant writing go so unnoticed, then here is the answer: politics, publishers, personality. All combined to cloak Sanford's career in anonymity.

And yet, even as that answer came clear, I realized that it was still not the right question.

I understood now the forces shaping John Sanford's writing life. The question had become how, in the absence of recognition, he had had the courage to believe, as he had, in his talent.

6.

When a writer fails, a presumption of guilt—not unlike that that attends rape victims—comes immediately into play, and first to be indicted is the virtue of the work. Obscurity, after all, is defined as a writer's failure to find an audience rather than an audience's failure to appreciate a writer. Let's not make the normal fuss about this situation: never has it not been true, never has it been truer than today. And still, let's not underestimate the problem: even the literary universes in Gissing's *Grub Street* and Balzac's *Illusions Perdues* had higher standards than today.

Viewed from this vantage, the career of John Sanford comes to emblematize a malaise that inhabits American literary life as never before.

But as that winter ended and I began to prepare the final draft of my own novel, the question he posed came to be a vaster one, perhaps the only question, in the end, that counted: What is it to be an artist? Ah, I thought to myself, as for the first time I recognized the nexus of Sanford's literary history and my own literary ambition. So that is the question.

Let me try to explain.

To publish a novel is to enter a world where a group of highly intelligent, highly motivated professionals—agents, editors, booksellers—enter the primary and hitherto private battleground of a writer, the battleground where he has try to wrestle his talent—such as that talent is—to the ground. From the moment of a manuscript's sale, that fundamental relationship is altered forever. Now it is not only a question of *realization* of one's talent, but of *recognition* by an audience. And so the private, often fierce ambition for realization becomes forever tied to an interdependency with that contingent, often deeply unfair process of recognition. For some, they become identical. This is what characterizes "mass market" writing, for which recognition—sales—is the only measure of success. For other writers—most, I think— the two goals are, to a greater or lesser degree, ever at odds. At the other extreme, more and more common today, as mainstream publishers shrink their literary lists, are writers for whom recognition halts realization, for they are no longer able to publish and, therefore, cease to write.

From this perspective, Sanford's literary career can be read as an absolute refusal to let his lack of recognition—by editors, reviewers, and readers—alter his steady, lifelong quest to realize his art. And alongside that determination, Sanford's autobiography stands as the record of an absolute refusal to let any judgment—religious, parental, critical, professional, or political—alter his sense of what is right.

What kind of person refuses, then, to bow to the pressure of the United States government, endures ignominy and ostracism, risks any security, and never wavers? What kind of person refuses to accept the judgment—any judgment—of others? And what does such a person have to teach us about writing at the end of the twentieth century? Was this, then, the question? By the time I had found and read just about everything Sanford had written, I had finished my own second novel, a highly political fictionalization of a Diane Wakoski poem in the guise of a mystery that was sure to please nobody, and yet which was exactly what I had wanted—and needed—to write. The suffocation of the situation, professionally and creatively, was intense. Like many writers, I was writing to an audience I hoped to create but being sold to an audience my publisher thought already existed, and in the contradiction between the two imperatives I did not see much chance of either of us succeeding. On vacation, that summer, I watched my daughter diving to the bottom of a swimming pool, then floating, face expectantly up, bubbles of laughter streaming from her mouth. I thought that what was ahead of me was just the same: I would be pushed to the bottom of a pool by my publisher, by my reviewers, and all I could do was hope that, like my daughter, I would float up before my air ran out, break surface, and write. I longed for some kind of guidance, and I knew that if I could answer the questions John Sanford posed to me, or rather, if I could figure out precisely what those questions were, I might find a way to face what was ahead.

One day I wrote to Sanford, telling him of my admiration for his work and asking if I could come out to tape an interview with him. And after an exchange of letters in which Sanford attempted to dissuade me, the way a rabbi is supposed to refuse three times a request to convert to Judaism, at last he agreed to my visit. And so, on a January morning, I was driving the Pacific Coast Highway to Santa Barbara to visit Mr. Sanford.

7.

The house where Sanford has lived since the fifties is set in a sloping garden. Two doors offer themselves on either end of a curving staircase. For a long time I stood outside by my car, listening to the birds in the trees.

I thought of the story my mother used to tell. I thought of Hawthorne's line: "Stay, Wakefield. Would you go to the sole home that is left you? Then step into your grave!" At last, the minute hand on my watch edging past ten, I knocked on the upper door. When that produced no response, I tried the lower, and from the cool, shaded interior a man nearing a hundred years old emerged, unaided, and ushered me in.

Inside, I found myself in a book-lined room with a couple of couches and armchairs surrounding a fireplace. Sanford returned to the seat from which I had evidently drawn him, in front of a black manual typewriter. He was five foot eight or so, a cogent, energetic, erudite person. Only his eyes, which are hard to describe, told me I was looking into the beginning of the twentieth century; only his eyes and the unnerving sense, which I have had before with people lucky enough to grow old with lucidity, that his interior reality, largely composed of incidents predating my birth, was much more real to him than I. For a time I fiddled with my tape recorder. But I knew Sanford did not want to be recorded and, suddenly, I knew I did not want to record him.

We talked for an hour, I trying to phrase the questions I had come to ask, he evading them with a gentleness I knew to be generous, for he had no answers for me. I asked him about rejection and he pulled from a drawer a list many pages long of the rejections a single one of his novels had received. I asked where he found the courage to appear as an unfriendly witness before HUAC and he dismissed the question by belittling his own courage and expressing sharp contempt—"Finks!"—for those who testified, as if there had never been any option other than the one he chose. I asked how he wrote in the face of criticism and he told me that he did not know how he wrote, that he sat to write and emerged some time later having written and without knowing how. Often he seemed to leave my presence entirely as he gazed with his hard-to-describe eyes into the past. And with each word I felt the pearlish moments slipping away, bringing me to the point when this unique hour of my life was going to end.

After some time he showed me Roberts's collected screenplays, on his shelves, written in the old double-column style with action on one side of the page and dialogue on the other. I asked, and he found in his carefully filed lifetime of correspondence a letter, written on thin blue airmail paper in elegant script, from his uncle Dave.

Upstairs, he served me coffee and cake in a kitchen that seemed untouched since the fifties: coffee percolator, Sara Lee cake, ungrounded sockets in the walls. We talked about his neighbors and his extended family, of whom only second cousins survived—with the exception of his sister Ruth, who lived in Los Angeles. Now that he had seen me, he allowed little Yiddishisms to come into his speech. More than anything else, he talked about his wife, a formidable and beautiful person whose picture was everywhere throughout the house, as is her presence everywhere in his writing. Roberts and he, I knew, had decided to have no children; he had a housekeeper, but she was away. I asked him if I could see some of the photographs of his family and he brought out an album containing, on the first page, a picture I knew from one of the first scenes of his autobiography:

> On the lawn of a hotel in the Catskills, your father, with you on his arm, is standing before a tree, and seated on a chair close by, your mother is inclined toward him, so that her head appears to be resting against the arm that's holding you. The years have made the print fade from black and white to bisque and brown, and the sky has turned to beige.
>
> Lines once sharp have lost their edge and forms their definition, and in the distance a group who seem to be watching a game or a display may in truth be doing nothing, may merely have chanced to gather where they'd live beyond their lives in sun and umber shade.
>
> You study yourself, a year-old boy in a sailor suit, with small dark-dot eyes staring at the camera, and you realize that he's gazing straight at you from the other end of the century. He's there on a mountain lawn that slopes toward Schoharie Creek, he's there between your father and your mother, he's breathing sachet powder and clear Havana smoke, he's hearing the voices, the laughter, the birds of 1905—he's doing what you're doing, peering through time at you.
>
> You wonder what he saw in the recesses of the lens, the bellows, the picture-taker's hood, whether he was pleased with what you'd made of him, whether the frown he wears is for some failure of yours, a wrong road travelled or the right one missed. You peer back through the hood, the bellows, the lens, and try to find a little-boy mind, but he stops you with those constant eyes, and all you learn is how you looked in the summer of 1905.

I knew then that I would never have an answer to how this man had faced down blacklisting and obscurity, bad reviews and, worse, no reviews, the temptations of Hollywood and the frustrations of nearly constant critical misunderstanding, and still, over a lifetime, followed his art to its highest realization, leaving a beautiful and pure collection of writing, a fully realized body of work, a testament to the highest power of art. I knew then that the processes of writing, real writing, are too intimately tied to the processes of being human for the questions I had come to ask.

The person would never tell me anything that the art could not, and the art would never reveal the depth of courage and fear of its production. Visiting Sanford, I thought that perhaps nothing can ever mitigate, ever help the harsh work of being a writer, and that perhaps that is no matter because, in the end, a writer's success or failure is of concern only to himself. And perhaps not even that. For perhaps writing is ultimately not production but practice; perhaps, as Diane Wakoski wrote:

> **Poetry is our history.**
> **We study the stars**
> **to understand temperatures.**
> **Life and death are the only issues;**
> **we often forget that—**
> **arranging our furniture,**
> **washing our cars.**

When I left Mr. Sanford's house, for a long time I drove aimlessly around Santa Barbara. I wanted a drink, but in the center of town the theme bars and restaurants were crowded with tanned, cheerful tourists; on the outskirts, wide, anonymous streets were populated only sparsely with Mexican workers. After a time I stopped at a phone booth and called home to New York, listening with sudden longing to the sounds of my children's voices, and behind them that of my wife, and behind them those of my mother and father, who must have been visiting: a tiny cacophony sounding enormously in my ear under the empty Pacific sky of sun.

After I hung up the phone I climbed back in my rental car and gunned its massive engine up the back way to Los Angeles, through the hills. For a time I drove thoughtlessly, enthralled by the road, taking the mad curves up to Ojai in big sweeps of my straight arms. And only when the road straightened did the clamor of grief begin. My car swerved up into the Santa Ynez mountains, the Pacific fell away behind, and I told myself bitterly, it is time, it is time to start finding the right questions.

. . . . . .

Following is an excerpt from John Sanford's forthcoming novel, A Palace of Silver.

.o. A PALACE OF SILVER .o.

Near one end of the Santa Barbara beach rises a hill called Bellosgarda, and spreading over its rounds is a cemetery. From the grounds, no part of the city can be seen; the view is of mountains inland and the Channel seaward, an expanse of some twenty miles to a chain of islands lying lavender along the horizon. Here and there, a cypress casts a filigree of shadow on the grass, and down in the hollows liveoaks grow. Headstones are few, the new custom being a tablet of metal or marble set flush with the sward, and rows of these curve with the concaves of the hill. Winding roadways cut the reserve into irregular sections, one of which runs along a cliff that rears from the water's edge. This land's-end place seems to be bounded only by sea and sky, and what sound can be heard there is made by the wind, the surf, and, if rain has fallen, the shrill of sea-birds come to probe the softened earth.

In one of the rows near the cliff, a bronze

plaque carries this inscription:

>MARGUERITE A. SANFORD
>1905-1989
>JOHN SANFORD
>1904-

Ten years have passed since it was embedded in her grave, and its components of copper, tin, and zinc have begun to give it a dapple of brown and green. In days to come, this will deepen almost to the color of the turf, but by then you too will be under the memento, and it will be others, if others ever come here, who remark on the patina and read the mottled names. Ten years have passed, but she remains; time has flowed around her, a fixture in a running stream.

"I'm glad I changed my mind, Johnny."
"About what?"
"Having our ashes put in the Channel. It was a foolish notion."
"Why foolish?"
"Don't you see? We'd've gotten separated, and I don't want that. I want to be with you."
"You loved your father and mother dearly. Why not with them?"
"Johnny, you're my husband."

.o.

Over the course of half a year, she'd suffered recurrent chest pain, a symptom of arterial blockage, and on each occasion she'd spent several days in the hospital. She was there again now, this time for a pacemaker to regulate the rhythm of her heart, and in her room just before she was taken to Surgery, you reached across her bedrail to stroke her hair. It'd long since gone gray, but never had you <u>thought</u> of it as gray, and when arranged to your liking, it revealed her ears, the most shapely you'd ever seen...And then an orderly came and wheeled her away.

Following as far as the waitingroom next to Surgery, you idled through a magazine, your mind elsewhere - on a small, trim being, fifty years your wife, but in your eyes still the girl of days gone by and still possessed of her winning ways. Still, you thought - and she was eighty-three! Rarely did you dwell on her age, and though you knew her date of birth as well as she, it'd been little more than numbers and a name.

But for once, you found it imperative, demanding to be heard abd understood, and what it told you was that your girl, lovely still, was old. Old, you thought, and with the word, another sought a hearing, ailing, and then a third, this one so direful that you strove to deny it. As to Maggie, even so late in her illness, you couldn't allow that she might be in danger, that in a nearby room something might be going wrong, that her readings might be dwindling or growing, that she might at that very moment...and you listened for telltale sound in the corridor, for commands, collisions, the rush of racing feet, for someone coming to say I'm sorry, Mr. Sanford...but it was your sped-up heart that you heard, your fearful self...At length, someone did come, but only with word that Maggie had been returned to her room.

When you joined her, she quickly dismissed you to go about your business, which you knew was there and nowhere else. At her urging, though, you left for home, saying that you'd come back again in the afternoon. But you have little memory of how you whiled away, the hours that intervened, for dread was still upon you, and it beclouded whatever you may have done. You may have wandered about the house, opening doors only to close them, you may have eaten without tasting, read without comprehension, or simply stared at a wall - or you may have done nothing, you may have done nothing at all...But vaguely through disquiet, you knew that you were seeking what mightn't be there one day, the presence, the life that gave life to the air.

In the afternoon, you returned to the hospital, and once more you were told yo go home. It was a ten-mile drive to your house in Montecito, and hardly were you inside when the telephone rang. Answering it, you heard a voice say <u>Mrs. Sanford is having a heart attack</u> - and though it took you only a quarter of an hour to reach the hospital, you arrived too late to see her alive. But in fancy, she seemed to be just then going, dying in the act of saying goodbye - to you, it could only be to you. Her eyes half-open, she was taking a last look at you, and she wwas speaking softly, with the last of her breath. You took up her hand and kissed its mist-smooth palm, and you kissed her mouth, still as fresh as falling rain, and you wept at the thought that this was all you'd ever know of it, that her special flavor would go with her into the grave. More than once hsd you said <u>I hate to see you leave a room</u> - but she was leaving this one, and the room of the world as well.

It was almost evening when you came away from the hospital, and for the third time that day, you drove back to your home - but it was a home no longer. It was a still life now, and you stood among the equivalents of flowers, fruit, and gunned-down game-birds. For half a century, you and Maggie had been acquiring objects, these things of wood and metal, of leather and paper and glass - books, rugs, china, bedside tables, illustration for the walls - the collect of a marriage - but it was bereft now and still-life dead. Her relics wrung you as you scanned them: she'd rested there, on that sofa, and that's the afghan you brought her when you thought her cold; those are her slippers beside the bed, that's the Tiffany she read by, and from a crystal flute, she'd given you a health in wine. These cubic spaces had known her voice, her laugh, her fragrance, and it anguished you that they'd know her rare company no more. But most painful, most piercing, was a sight of what she'd worn. Her wardrobe spoke of her shipshape figure, and you seemed to see it again in a suit, a dress, a blouse, a jacket, and you touched one and another as though to find her rounds through the fabric, but her cordial dimensions were gone, leaving only the clothing she once had adorned.

"Someone could use it. Why don't you give it away?"
"But it'd be like giving you away."
"It isn't me. It's only old clothes, and getting older."
"I was with you for everything you

ever bought."
"Sometimes I wasn't there. I remember a robe you brought home from Bullock's. I wore it for twenty years before throwit away."
"I saved it."
"You did? Why?"
"You'd worn it for twenty years...."

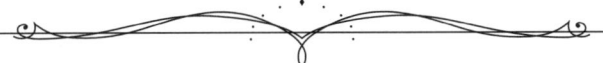

Something hidden. Go and find it. Go and look behind the Ranges—
Something lost behind the Ranges. Lost and waiting for you. Go!

— *The Explorer,* by Rudyard Kipling, 1903

LOST AND FOUND™

THE LOST BROTHER
FRANK BURES

V. S. Naipaul won the war of sibling rivalry on the battleground of fame and letters. But was his younger brother Shiva the better writer?

Sir Vidia Naipaul's shadow is long and dark, and in it, somewhere, you will find mention of a younger brother, Shiva, a writer who now is all but lost to the world.

Shiva Naipaul was only five when his brother Vidia (known as V. S.) left Trinidad to study at Oxford. Growing up, Shiva knew him only by his voice on the BBC and the things he left behind. To Shiva, V.S. was a "notional being," a doppelganger who plagued him with impossibly high expectations.

Yet somehow, he met them and climbed aboard a ship for Oxford, triumphant winner of his own Island Scholarship. It was Shiva's first unwitting step on the path already taken by his brother—the road to being a writer.

Shiva's first novel, *Fireflies,* won three awards (the John Llewelyn Rhys Memorial Prize, the Winifred Holtby Memorial Prize, and the Jock Campbell New Statesman Award). His second, *The Chip-Chip Gatherers,* won the first-ever Whitbread Literary Award. Both are bittersweet comedies set on Trinidad.

But there was a deeper angst pushing Shiva out into the world, which could not

Shiva Naipaul in 1980, by Jerry Bauer

if you prefer, obsessions. What do terms like 'liberation,' 'revolution,' 'socialism,' actually mean to the people—i.e., the masses—who experience them?"

The chronicle of his six-month trip through Kenya, Tanzania, and Zambia, *North of South: An African Journey,* is filled with moments of sadness and humor, themes that underpin nearly all his work. Tragedy and comedy were the yin and yang of his world. Here he is on a bus in Tanzania:

"I was sinking into my usual trancelike state when I was awakened by a sudden grinding of brakes, the unmistakable thud of metal impinging on yielding flesh, followed by a tumbling forward of the passengers standing in the aisle. A great gabbling commotion broke out on all sides. I soon discovered what had happened: we had hit a wandering cow."

Shiva wrote across the world—about the Bush Negros of Surinam, the Rastafari of Jamaica, the politics of India, the budding New Age in California. This last stemmed from his search for the roots of Jonestown, Guyana, and the mass suicide of the fol-

be satisfied through fiction alone—a need to see if things were really as they seemed and to show when they weren't—a need he shared with his brother.

This urge first sent Shiva to East Africa. He wanted to see the effects of colonialism and independence. In a book proposal to his editor, he explained: "The book will arise, I hope, out of my own concerns—or,

lowers of Jim Jones in 1978, leading to his book *Journey to Nowhere: A New World Tragedy*.

"The tone, the vocabulary, were unmistakable," he wrote of a pamphlet for the New Earth Exposition. "'Interrelatedness. Human. Fragile balance. Life-style.' The handout spoke in the unique accents of California. I had been living in San Francisco long enough to have become almost inured to the singular blend of eco and ego, of technologically minded worldliness and etherealism, of overripe self-consciousness and opulent complacency."

The observation, made twenty years ago, remains deeply relevant (echoes of Heaven's Gate), as does all of Shiva's writing about the world and human ties.

There are two strands that run through his seven books. They were perhaps best described by Ryszard Kapuscinski in his review of *Beyond the Dragon's Mouth*, a collection of stories and travel pieces. "Much of Naipaul's writing," he wrote, "has a tone that can be described, paradoxically, as one of sad humor."

In 1985, Shiva Naipaul had plans for another novel and was working on a new book about Australia. But near the end of chapter 3 he got up from his typewriter and fell over, dead from a heart attack at age forty.

There were tributary footnotes in *Time* and *Newsweek*. But in general, no one eulogized and no one seemed to notice.

Today, V. S. Naipaul continues to enjoy whispers of a Nobel Prize, while Shiva, who was at least his equal as a writer, seems ever more lost in the darkness of his brother's shadow.

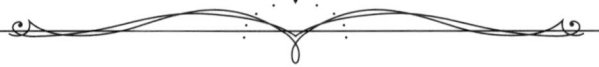

LOST AND FOUND

Robert Ruark's
The Honey Badger

Here's how you walked out on your wife in the early fifties if you were a big-time novelist like Alec Barr and you were just good and goddamned tired of her pansy decorator pals flitting around and you could not—simply could not—bring yourself to go to the Hazeltine's dinner party. You stalk out of your Upper East Side apartment and check into a shabby-genteel hotel where the clerk comments insinuatingly on your absence of luggage. You head over to Toots Shor's, where you tie one on with—but don't sleep with—an old flame from newspapering days. The next day you work off your ghastly hangover by walking all the way to Yankee Stadium through Spanish Harlem (where the Puerto Ricans hiss *maricon* at you from the stoops). There you watch the great DiMaggio break a seventeen-game hitless streak with a triple—capped off with a friendly wink in your direction. So you come to your senses and check out of the fleabag hotel and into the Ritz-Carlton, where you should have gone in the first damned place. And you tell the clerk, whose name you almost remember, the following:

I want a suite. I want a very big suite. And I want to be semi-incognito for a few days. I haven't a stitch with me, so I want your best valet to go to Brooks and pick me up half a dozen shirts, two pairs of pajamas, a half-dozen pairs of black socks, the same number of shorts, and two or three plain black neckties. I'll also require some shaving tackle, toothpaste, toothbrushes—hard—deodorant—you know, the complete drill. I'll ring up Mr. Florian at Brooks and tell him your man's coming, and settle a couple of details. They have all my measurements.

It has been more than thirty years since I read this passage from Robert Ruark's *The Honey Badger* as a teenager—bookish and utterly clueless. And, as pathetic as it is to admit, I thought this was just tremendously cool. (I

BY
GERALD
HOWARD

still can't go into Brooks without wanting to put my measurements on file.) I took this and numerous other scenes just dripping with self-importance and self-pity to be the straight gen on the male prerogative and the mysteries of adult life. It was my personal equivalent of *Valley of the Dolls*: the overheated second-rate novel that for a time served as my road map to the glamorous future.

Robert Ruark was an influential columnist for the Scripps-Howard chain in the forties and fifties and the author of two wide-screen novels of the Mau-Mau uprisings, *Uhuru* and *Something of Value*. Think of him as a Hemingway who never went to Paris and met Gertrude Stein, a hairy-chested litterateur without modernist discipline or aesthetic intent, but with every posturing impulse intact and sending. *The Honey Badger,* published in 1965, was his final book, a 569-page compendium of every reigning midcentury cliché about the male American novelist and the castrating American she-bitch. For Ruark's alter-ego Alec Barr, life came down, time and again, to a choice between the woman or the typewriter. The title says it all: the honey badger "kills for malice and for sport, and it does not go for the jugular—it goes straight for the groin. It has a hell of a lot in common with the modern American woman."

Nothing in my experience of either sex or the publication of fiction has borne out a single one of Robert Ruark's assertions about the rutting or the writing life. So why does this self-aggrandizing exercise in bad John O'Hara-ism stick so vividly in my brain, and why do I remember it—and I mean all of it—

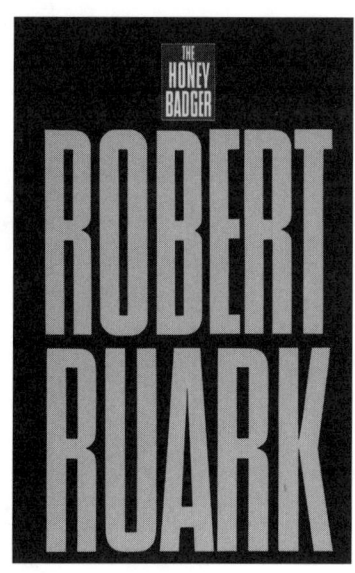

with such wry affection? In part it was because the book proposed a vivid portrait of metropolitan sophistication just across the river from my colorless Brooklyn neighborhood, which I was so anxious to escape. But when I think of *The Honey Badger* now, I am reminded of the final scene of *Son of Kong*—the dumb beast about to be drowned by the floodwaters of cultural change, marshaling one last gesture of futile yet perversely inspiring defiance before they close over his head. We leave Alec Barr contemplating the prospects of prostate cancer, and it isn't pretty; meanwhile, that genuine alpha male of American literature, Norman Mailer, was about to be stalked on the cultural veldt by Germaine Greer and be taken as a prisoner of sex. Susan Faludi wept.

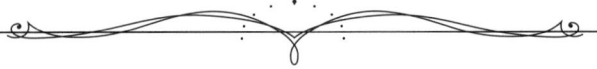

LOST AND FOUND

Michael Edwards's
Priscilla, Elvis and Me: In the Shadow of the King

BY ROBERT POLITO

Inadvertence—ordinarily the predilection of surrealists and cranks—also spikes the most plangent as-told-to books and celebrity (or almost-celebrity) memoirs. Remove "Michael Edwards" from the title page and substitute "Don DeLillo," "Vladimir Nabokov," or even "Ford Madox Ford," and *Priscilla, Elvis and Me: In the Shadow of the King* emerges as an audacious, slyly sad novel of accidental confession.

Edwards announces himself as "the most successful male model in the United States and Europe," although memory and a casual poll of friends suggest that he was no more prominent back in 1988, when *Priscilla, Elvis and Me* appeared. His story proposes to chronicle his seven-year grand passion for Priscilla Presley, yet Edwards keeps stumbling over his disclosures. On their first meeting, he passes out on her suede couch. "I think you're familiar with the living room," she reminds him a few days later. On their next date, an outing with Lisa Marie's friends to Magic Mountain, he vomits the beer he drank behind the Spin of Death. "I watched Priscilla and the girls climb onto the ride and, for the first time since childhood, I felt joy," Edwards concludes. He falls for Priscilla after he hears her dial random telephone numbers, pretending she's a hooker. "Something about it touched a place in my heart, and I felt the first stirrings of love for her that evening."

But Priscilla ultimately proves an inconvenient nullity—any sensation of an actual woman atomizes in his fury at her stint on *Dallas* ("she had found a new fascination—herself"). His self-consuming ardor roosts elsewhere, inside the ghost of Elvis Presley and the body of the King's look-alike daughter. Successively aggrandized and shamed by "my position as Elvis's successor," Edwards steadily derails. "A very big Elvis" visits him in a dream, disguised as God: "I realized Elvis's spirit had never left. Priscilla and Lisa were still under his protection, and Elvis was still waiting for the right someone to come along." Elvis soon invades every recess of his waking life, from his meals ("As I sat and stuffed myself, I imagined this is how Elvis must have lived") to his career ("Elvis must have felt exasperated, mass-producing all those fluff movies.... I'd felt the same way on many occasions modeling clothes") to Priscilla's infidelities ("Now I know how Elvis had felt when he caught Priscilla"). Edwards flees Elvis's monogrammed, gold-framed sunglasses on his way to Priscilla's bed, then appropriates his old cologne. He even purchases his mother a Cadillac.

For his creepiest substitution, Edwards reaches a startling equation: Priscilla was to Elvis as Lisa Marie is to him. Picking Lisa up at Catholic school, he lingers over her wool skirt, white blouse, and loafers—the young Priscilla had worn "a uniform just like Lisa's.... I could certainly understand Elvis's feelings.... it definitely turned him on." He scarcely can conceal his erection as they play together in the pool and, after a quarrel with Priscilla, Edwards drunkenly lurches into Lisa's room. "I wanted someone to talk to, but Lisa was asleep. I lifted a corner of the sheets and gazed at her. She was lying on her back, and her honey-colored hair was spread out over the pillow. She was my beloved, and I couldn't even tell her.... Everything about her was exactly what I wanted in a woman." Lisa Marie is thirteen.

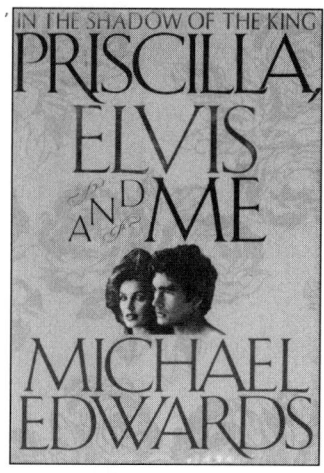

Priscilla, Elvis and Me traces the arc of a rent-boy *Lolita*: Michael Edwards as Humbert Humbert, Priscilla as Charlotte Haze, Lisa Marie as Lolita, and Elvis as the spoiling Quilty. But refuse the temptation to spin Edwards's tale into camp—he's too strange, too chilling for that. As another Elvis recently sang, "Stop me if you've heard this alibi." ∎

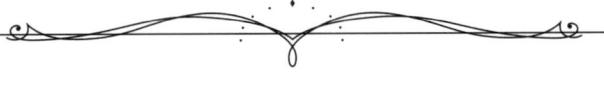

LOST AND FOUND

David Bradley's
The Chaneysville Incident

When David Bradley's *The Chaneysville Incident* was published in 1981, the novel was a sensation among academics and literary critics, earning the second-ever PEN/Faulkner Award for fiction. At the time, Bradley was hailed as a new major force in African-American literature. Critics compared him to James Baldwin and Ralph Ellison. Bradley was only thirty-one, and *Chaneysville* was supposed to be the launch pad of his brilliant career. Instead, both he and the book now live on the margins of the literary landscape.

Chaneysville, like many great works by African-American writers, is a novel that features a search at its center. John Washington, a young black man who teaches "white" history at a Philadelphia university, is summoned home to rural Pennsylvania to care for the dying Jack Crawley: his late father's best friend, John's de facto guardian when he was a child, and the family's unofficial storyteller.

John hasn't been home in years, and upon his return he must confront the ghosts of his family's past, including his father's mysterious death. That story, however, is intertwined with "the Chaneysville Incident"—the story of thirteen runaway slaves who, as they were about to be recaptured, were shot dead and were subsequently buried in thirteen thoughtfully, lovingly laid-out graves.

Complicating matters is John's relationship, back in Philadelphia, with Judith, a white psychiatrist whose roots can be traced back to Virginia slave owners. In a lesser writer's hands, John and Judith's story could have easily devolved into a litany of clichés about the troubles interracial couples face. Bradley, however, deftly captures the complexities and nuances of their relationship, and of

BY
JOHN
FREDERICK
MOORE

John's ambivalent relations with white people in general.

Chaneysville is effective on many levels—family saga, personal journey, history, love story—yet it is Bradley's forceful, energetic prose that propels the book forward. The opening paragraph fairly leaps off the page:

> **Sometimes you can hear the wire, hear it reaching out across the miles; whining with its own weight, crying from the cold, panting at the distance, humming with the phantom sounds of someone else's conversation. You cannot always hear it—only sometimes; when the night is deep and the room is dark and the sound of the phone's ringing has come slicing through uneasy sleep; when you are lying there, shivering, with the cold plastic of the receiver pressed tight against your ear. Then, as the rasping of your breathing fades and the hammering of your heartbeat slows, you can hear the wire: whining, crying, panting, humming, moaning like a live thing.**

At the end of *Chaneysville*, John's discovery of the fate of the runaway slaves offers a sense of hope and a testament to the essential goodness of humanity that few novels (sadly enough) about the African-American experience provide. Think of the outrage that permeates Richard Wright's *Native Son*, or the melancholy of Toni Morrison's *Beloved*. There's a lot of bitterness and regret in *Chaneysville*, to be sure, but the conclusion demonstrates that even in a society built upon hate and bondage, there is room for decency—an essential *rightness* that can't be explained for any reason other than that, when given the chance, people will do the decent thing.

Here is a book that deserves to be considered one of the great works of late-twentieth-century American literature, alongside DeLillo and Pynchon, as well as African-American classics like *Invisible Man* and *Song of Solomon*. So why, in less than twenty years, has *Chaneysville* slipped through the cracks?

Part of the reason is that Bradley did not follow up *Chaneysville*. He didn't exactly leave without a trace, publishing articles and reviews in national publications, and for the longest time there was talk of an upcoming book-length essay, *On Race and Racism*, which was finally published in September 1999 by Viking Penguin.

Bradley has striking things to say on racism in the new book, though it's hard to imagine he could make his point any better than he did in *Chaneysville*. With any luck, *On Race and Racism* will bring new attention to his lost classic.

LOST AND FOUND

Robert Paul Smith's
Where Did You Go? Out. What Did You Do? Nothing.

We are still following the long, unfading fashion in childhood memoir that has marked American nonfiction for years. Much of it is an exercise of imagination rather than memory—so many perfectly reconstructed conversations, so many vibrantly detailed early scenes. Modern memoir is also often a terrible place, full of pain and loss and terror. It makes for good stories. But good stories alone don't make memoirs; when I read this new school of remembrance, I rarely hear the voices of real children. Children are serious but rarely dour, full of faith and cant, passionate, fragile creatures with simple words and complex beliefs. They are great narrators, among the most difficult of narrators to create, far more difficult than our own hindsighted, wistful voice.

There is a real child's voice in my cherished first edition of Robert Paul Smith's childhood memoir, *Where Did You Go? Out. What Did You Do? Nothing.* It was published in 1957, the year I was born. I inherited it from my mother.

It is long out of print and far out of fashion. There is no terror here. Smith writes with languorous ease, relaxed, unhurried, about vacant lots, mumblety-peg, school punishments, the glorious uses of clothesline, Indian wrist burns, chestnut killers, and treehouses. But the small miracle of his prose is that when you read these quiet scenes, you are not hearing the voice of the writer remembering the past. *You* are remembering.

> **Lying awake at night, knuckling my eyeballs so that I could see the flashes of light, the fireworks that only I knew about. Taking off the rubber band that I had wrapped around my thumb, tight, so that I could feel the prickles, the electricity, the exquisite torture of the slow removal of the garter. Going to sleep with my right big toe in my left hand, my right arm wrapped around my head holding the lobe of my left ear, to find out if I would wake up that way in the morning.**

BY SALLIE TISDALE

He remembers, and respects, the rules of children, their losses, their dreams, their wisdom. These are losses no greater than getting knocked over by a big kid for your lunch money or being sent unjustly to the cloakroom. Dreams no bigger than being "Tarzanoftheapes," or meeting one of the women in a stolen copy of the *Police Gazette,* or getting a Shetland pony "as soon as we had sold thirty-four million packages of blueing." Rules about who's bigger and who's stronger and when it's okay to steal lumber. The Law—that is, what grownups make you do, for reasons of their own—was a distant and overarching structure, but not exactly local. Smith knows (and doesn't bother to say so because to him it is so obvious) that kids' rules are big rules and their dreams are big dreams, but private ones. Their wisdom ranges from superstition to the supernatural, and fills the universe with questions you cannot ask a grownup. (What's really inside a golf ball, anyway? Will it explode? Dare we find out? I dare you.) Smith knows that childhood is a dangerous, exciting country ("If you cut yourself in the web of skin between your thumb and forefinger, you die. That's it. No ifs or buts. Cut. Die.") and that no one can teach children about it better than other children.

I think we were right about grownups being the natural enemies of kids. We knew that what they wanted us to do was to be like them. And that was for the birds.

"Pop, look at this. It's a pollywog, look at it." "Um," said your father. Other kids said, "Jeez, where'd you get it? Are there any more? What'll you take for it?"

"Hey, mother, you know what? Ted Fenster's kid brother eats dirt." "Well, don't let me catch you doing it," said your mother. "Go-wan," a kid would say. "Eats dirt? You mean, really eats dirt? Yer full of it." "He'll do it for a penny," you said, and you went off to find Ted Fenster's kid brother, and by God, he ate dirt, lots of it, spoonfuls of it, for a penny.

Years ago, I wrote a wistful, short review of this book for another magazine and, lo and behold, a month or two later a package came in the mail. It was an old copy of the collected novels of Robert Paul Smith, sent with a lovely thank-you note from his son, who was raised right. When I was a kid, I didn't do most of the things Smith describes—play his games, read his comics, chant his songs. But what I did, I did in the same way, looking out at the world from the same wondering place, which is the whole universe for a long, long time. Find this book and then curl up on an old couch on a summer afternoon and don't get up until you're done.

LOST AND FOUND

Alex Abella's
The Killing of the Saints

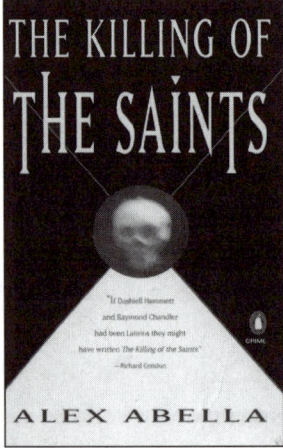

Having been intimately involved with this country's criminal-justice system, I tend to read a lot of crime fiction. Alex Abella's 1991 *Killing of the Saints* is one of the best crime-fiction books I've ever read. It starts with two Santeria Marliettos pulling a hot armed robbery that turns into a bloodbath. Told first person in a driving style with some of the sharpest dialogue ever put on the page, it follows a straight-shooting gumshoe, Charlie, as he unravels the truth about who was behind the bungled robbery.

Abella weaves Santeria into the story so deeply that you can feel the beat of the drums and the smell of the sacrificial blood. A Cuban refugee who has worked in the mess that is the criminal-justice system, Abella brings a realism and conviction to his work that is lacking in all the other legal/crime novels I've read. He shows the deal making and double-crossing that is the so-called justice system, does it so well that you can almost feel the desperation and hypocrisy rising from the pages.

Characters in big-name crime books tend to be either clearly good or clearly bad, but Abella's people are a disturbing combination of good and bad; strong and weak. Like Hammett, who brings a burning moral ambiguity to his flatfoot, the Continental Op, Abella's Charlie is as complex as any real human being. As capable of villainy as nobility.

As Charlie descends into the surreal, violent Santeria world, Abella implicates the reader, drawing you in so that you find yourself evaluating what really constitutes good and evil, making you take a good look at yourself and the world we live in. All the while entertaining the hell out of you.

BY EDDIE LITTLE

Three Poems

by

Yehuda Amichai

Translated by Chana Bloch and Chana Kronfeld

All the Motions and Positions

All the motions and the positions in my body—
it's already been done.
I sit on a chair and think like Rodin's Thinker.
Ever since I sat folded up in my mother's belly,
I have carried inside me the wisdom of the folding chair.
My arms are raised like Moses' arms when he raised the Tablets of the Law,
my arms are raised without holding a thing,
a bit in disbelief, a bit in despair.
I give hugs like King David on the roof, or helpless hugs
like Jesus on the cross, but the palms of my hands
are free, I am free, though everything
has already come to pass. I have learned to swim
in the stream of consciousness, and I know a thing or two
about the difference between wire and wireless, God and
No-God, jet and chopper, a door
that opens and closes with a slam
and a revolving door that keeps revolving.

Life is Called Life

1.

Life is called life as the west wind is called
west, though it blows toward the east.
The way death is called death, though it blows toward life.
In a cemetery we remember the living, and outside it—
the dead. As the past leads to the future
though it's called past, as you to me and I to you in love
though I'm called by my name and you by yours.
As spring provides for summer, as summer beds down into fall.
As my thoughts will be till the end of my life. That is the banner of my God.

2.

Each day now I hear the circles of my life closing,
the click of buckles, like kisses
of conciliation and love. And these lend a rhythm
to the final version of my life. Things that were lost long ago
find their places now, like billiard balls, each one into its pocket.
Contracts and prophecies are fulfilled, prophecies true and false.
I come upon the missing lids of pots and pans that stayed uncovered,
I find the matching pieces, like an ancient contract of clay,
broken into two parts, unequal but fitting together.
Like a mosaic, like a jigsaw puzzle, children searching
for the missing pieces. When the game is over,
the picture will be whole. Complete.

And What is My Life Span?

1.

I've never been in those places where I've never been
and never will be, I have no share in the infinity of light-years and dark-years
but the darkness is mine, and the light, and my time
is my own. The sand on the seashore—those infinite grains
are the same sand where I made love in Achziv and Caesarea.
The years of my life I have broken into hours, and the hours into minutes
and seconds and fractions of seconds. These, only these,
are the stars above me
that cannot be numbered.

2.

And what is my life span? I'm like a man gone out of Egypt:
the Red Sea parts, I cross on dry land,
two walls of water, on my right hand and on my left.
Pharaoh's army and his horsemen behind me. Before me the desert,
perhaps the promised land, too. That is my life span.

3.

Open closed open. Before we are born, everything is open
in the universe without us. For as long as we live, everything is closed
within us. And when we die, everything is open again.
Open closed open. That's all we are.

4.

What then is my life span? Like shooting a self-portrait.

I set up the camera a few feet away on something stable

(the one thing that's stable in this world),

I decide on a good place to stand, near a tree,

run back to the camera, press the timer,

run back again to that place near the tree,

and I hear the ticking of time, the whirring

like a distant prayer, the click of the shutter like an execution.

That is my life span. God develops the picture

in His big darkroom. And here is the picture:

white hair on my head, eyes tired and heavy,

eyebrows black, like the charred lintels

above the windows in a house that burned down.

My life span is over.

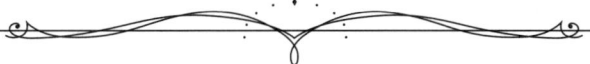

from 1972

NICHOLAS CHRISTOPHER

1.

Maya who weaves illusions

and casts the light from men's eyes—

the temptress of the *Dhammapada*—

turns down my bed in a suburb

of this factory town,

in the yellow house

with a caged canary in the foyer

and the shadow of a panther roaming the basement.

Maya who waits tables,

punches train tickets,

turns tricks,

who presses you to the floor

with her nipples brushing your lips

and her own lips parting slowly

on the empty vowel

that fills the mouths of those

with nothing to say, nothing to fear,

which strikes me—

thirsty at the crossroads

where a weather-stripped tree

offers the only shade—

to be one and the same.

2.

As the sun gilds the Arno and shades the stern faces

of the angels atop the cathedral,

two buses collide, toppling a statue of Machiavelli,

fire sweeps a school for the blind,

a nun finds an apple ripening on a pear tree.

At my hotel an old woman is crossing the lobby

in a shimmering dress

with a parrot on her shoulder

who is said to possess knowledge

of stars not yet born,

dreams not yet dreamed

crimes not yet committed.

After the hills darken and the torn clouds scatter,

the parrot ascends to a palm tree

in the mezzanine and begins squawking

names, dates, places—

his particular secret history of the living and the dead

that may never come to pass.

3.

The German film is dubbed in English with Greek subtitles

and after six rounds of raki

my companion for the night,

who speaks only French,

proclaims it a masterpiece.

Her fishhook earrings are baited with flashes of moonlight.

Her lipstick sparkles like rain.

At 2 a.m. at a discothèque by the sea

she kicks off one shoe, then the other,

drops the straps of her gold dress,

and tosses her hair from shoulder to shoulder

while dancing with other men

and with me

and then, finally, alone, her back against the wall.

Later she will surprise me.

Not in the alley, cloudy with the scent of hibiscus,

where we stop to neck in a cone of light,

or in bed, kicking off the blue sheets,

but on my balcony, gazing at the warships

anchored on the horizon, when, huddled naked,

an unlit cigarette between her lips,

she addresses me for the first time in perfect English.

The girl in that film who drowned said love is the only crime.

Understand—I am no criminal.

4.

A church filled with fiery flowers,

with widows in white and brides in black, milling.

At the midpoint of this broiling summer,

as waves of napalm crest in jungles

on the other side of the world

where every second someone is dying for nothing

while someone else is being sacrificed

in the name of something larger than himself,

I'm an island on an island

of two thousand living people

and five millennia of diaphanous souls

who have journeyed beyond the sun to become

(according to Hipparchus, himself born here)

stars, each of them, on the sphere that encloses

all things, including this girl dancing

along the seawall with bloodied feet,

trailing a fishnet delicate as lace,

the flame of her hair fanned by the wind

and her eyes bright as the candles

the mourners carry through the town at night,

every night,

down the same sequence of alleys

to the sea.

5.

A single star burns above a black palm.
The moon's rays spray over the mountain peaks,
across the orchards and the tall grass,
onto the cresting waves beyond the cove.
We'll stay here for three nights
before I drive north
and you sail farther south—
as far as you can go.
We'll never meet again,
but for years I will glimpse your reflection in mirrors—
in hotel rooms, restaurants, trains—
always the same downcast eyes and baleful smile
and the words I can never quite decipher
forming on your lips:
something you wanted to tell me,
or something that I longed to hear?
More likely, as happened in that place
with the solitary palm and its shadow—
creeping across the sand to be erased by the surf—
something that had nothing to do with me at all.

PILGRIMAGE™

THE DEVIL IS A POET

One of the world's leading poets finds that evil and innocence are inseparable in the art of Hieronymus Bosch.

Last May, on my first trip to Lisbon, I finally had the opportunity to see Bosch's *Temptation of St. Anthony*. On a rainy weekday morning, the Museu Nacional de Arte Antiga, a converted seventeenth-century palace, appeared closed. After my friend and I paid the admission in the dim lobby, we encountered no one, except for an occasional guard dozing off on his or her feet. It was so quiet in the museum, every time we stopped before a painting, we could hear ourselves breathe. The palace houses the world's largest collection of fifteenth- and six- teenth-century Portuguese paintings, muddy with age and badly in need of cleaning. We made our lengthy tour among what were mostly religious paintings, admiring a few works here and there, lingering for a while in the applied-arts wing before the marvelous Japanese screen showing a Portuguese delegation disembarking in Nagasaki in the sixteenth century, but finally we had to ask one of the women attendants as to the whereabouts of Bosch.

We crossed several cavernous rooms, the martyrs being tormented in the paintings seemingly as surprised by our

Charles Simic

sudden appearance as we were by theirs, and just as we began to suspect that we had misunderstood the directions we were given, there was the altarpiece, far larger than we expected it to be. The triptych was set up and slightly elevated on a kind of platform, well lit, newly cleaned, its reds, blues, and yellows bright and rich, the details vivid, the whole spectacle simply breathtaking. For a painting to still be able to shock after almost five centuries is no small accomplishment. How many other works of art can do that? We stood before it absolutely stunned, overwhelmed and supremely happy, thinking, There cannot be any other world but this. Surprisingly, all that feverish activity with its myriad of grotesque particulars in all three panels gave the impression of coherence and purpose. Of course, I had read enough about Bosch previously to know that the theological and philosophical meaning of this and most of his other paintings has remained elusive despite numerous attempts to solve their mystery; nevertheless, I could not escape the feeling that it all fits together and makes sense in some still unknown way.

Since not much is known about Bosch, except for the years of his life, c. 1450-1516, in the town of 's-Hertogenbosch in the Netherlands, speculations have ranged widely about the originality of his art. The sources of his iconography and his ideas have been sought in heretical and doomsday sects, alchemical practices, medieval diableries, astrology, and, most persuasively in my view, in bestiaries, fantastic travel books, and folklore. He has been called a mystic, a moralist, a satirist, a schizophrenic, and even a realist. The Black Plague, the pillage and massacres of the Hundreds Year War, and witch burnings, as well as the many of the horrors of our century, came to mind when I first saw the triptych. The extraordinary thing about Bosch is that his vision is somehow both old and modern. I was also reminded of Rimbaud's poem "Alchemy of the Verb,"

> **I accustomed myself to simple hallucinations. I would see quite clearly a mosque in place of a factory, a school of drummers made up of angels, carriages on the roads in the sky, a drawing room at the bottom of a lake; monsters, mysteries, a vaudeville billboard conjured up horrors in my path.**

> *He has been called a mystic, a moralist, a satirist, a schizophrenic, and even a realist.*

Wherever imagination has reigned supreme in art and literature since Goya and Blake, Bosch suggests himself as a predecessor.

All these and other associations, of course, came to me later. Facing the painting, I was simply trying to orient myself. The temptation of St. Anthony, I recalled, took place in the Egyptian desert, but what I saw before me was a mixture of various kinds of landscape with buildings from different historical periods. These ruined towers, tombs, and palaces looked like the stage set of some lost opera co-written by the Marquis de Sade. The temptation of holy men was a standard subject in Bosch's day, but while the tradition counted on a few devils, he made the whole of creation one huge hybrid creature, a demon, as it were, composed of human, animal, vegetable, and inanimate parts.

Exaggeration and distortion of features has always been the staple of comic image making, but Bosch did something else. He was a visionary collagist. He painted as if one could only get at reality by first chopping up everything and then reassembling it again. Like Lautréamont, who wrote in a poem, "beautiful as the encounter of a sewing machine and an umbrella on a dissecting table," he plays the game of joining seemingly unjoinable realities, making the results seem inevitable and leaving us to reconsider the meaning of representation. One of his earliest commentators, Fray Jose de Siguenza, said in 1605, "The difference, which, to my mind, exists between the pictures of this man and those of all others is that the others try to paint man as he appears on the outside, while he alone had the audacity to paint him as he is on the inside." In other words, the Spaniard regarded Bosch's grotesqueries as a form of naturalism.

In the meantime, there is the actual painting to feast one's eyes on. Its sky is thick with odd flying contraptions worthy of a Mad Max movie. Instead of brooms, human beings and devils are riding on fishes, birds, and sailing ships as if this were the most normal thing to do. One demon is doing a handstand on a flying scythe. A stork has the mast of a ship attached to its tail. St. Anthony is saying a prayer on a bullfrog, while next to him an incubus waves a branch with a few dry leaves left on it as if to whip him and make him go faster.

It's much worse down below. A village is on fire, the smoke darkening a portion of the sky. The army presumably responsible for it is trotting off merrily, their leader on a white horse. A great solemn allegorical procession of grotesque creatures winds across all three panels. They are dressed as men and women of rank who at first appear to be wearing carnival masks until one notices that their body parts belong to other species. Tree trunks, branches, even an earthen pot and many other unlikely items make up the rest of their bodies. One man wears an owl on his head, another an apple. Inside each being there are multiple monsters hiding, devouring each other or struggling to come out. Cruelty, folly, and lechery reign in every nook and cranny.

What caught my attention right off was the chapel in the central panel in which Jesus stands with his face turned toward us, apparently distracted from his prayer by the tumult outside. Incredibly, he has been praying to himself crucified on the cross. Next door, there's what looks like a Venetian palazzo. In a tent on its roof a monk and a

THE DEVIL IS A POET

woman are guzzling wine, while over their shoulders a naked woman is diving from the parapet into the canal, and another fat monk already undressed and with a towel over his shoulders is cautiously descending the steep steps, watched from inside the palace by a big old cow and a large bird carrying a tall ladder.

A kind of exhilaration came over me the more I studied the painting. As with the best images in Fellini's and Pasolini's films, or some outrageous comparison in a poem by Russell Edson or James Tate, I was delighted. There's no joy like the one a truly outrageous image on the verge of blasphemy gives. In Bosch, wickedness and innocence are constantly rubbing shoulders. To paint a true picture of the world, he seems to be saying, one needs to include both what people see with eyes open and what they see when they shut their eyes. He does not tell us which is which. For him, the visible and the invisible belong in the same landscape.

It took me a while to begin to pay attention to the saintly hermit and his story. In the left wing we see him helped on his way by

three companions, one of whom is Hieronymus himself. St. Anthony is weak from battling the fiends. They're crossing a small bridge underneath which a monk and a demonic creature are reading, a letter or perhaps a set of instructions about the next round of temptations. A birdlike messenger with a funnel on his head and skates on his feet is delivering a further missive. Over the saint's bowed head, a fish on wheels rolls over the ground carting a church steeple. A giant on all fours, right out of *Gulliver's Travels,* with a cloak of grass over his shoulders and an arrow sticking out of his forehead, stares dumbfounded at the goings-on in the sky. Up his rear end, in a small house almost crushed by his weight, there's the entrance to a brothel with a woman peeking out of the window on the lookout for customers.

I was also interested in the fellow with a black stovepipe hat and red robes casually lounging in the central panel with his back to us, who resembles the titular figure in Bosch's famous painting *The Conjurer.* Is he the director of this *theatrum mundi?* He calmly observes a pig-headed priest reading from a blue prayer book as if auditioning for a part, while a dead woman with a hollow tree for a bonnet and a living child clutched in her arms waits her turn. Does he understand what he has created, or is he as perplexed as we are? Behind his back, a huge tomatolike fruit has cracked open with ripeness. A horse-headed demon strumming a harp leads the way out of it, riding on a plucked goose that wears boots and inside whose severed neck another animal-like face is peeking out.

Each one of us is a synthesis of the real and unreal. We all wear a guise. Even within our own minds, we make constant efforts to conceal ourselves from ourselves, only to be repeatedly found out. Bosch did not need Freud or Jung to tell him that our inner lives are grotesque and scandalous. He also knew something they did not. The world inside us is comic. Bosch's paintings cannot be understood without appreciating their riotous humor.

Satan pulled every trick out of his infernal bag, and still the saint went on praying. He saw himself surrounded by a swarm of nightmarish creatures and harems of naked women and his composure did not leave him. Finally, Satan dispatched his own wife. In the right wing we see her play bawdy peek-a-boo at the entrance to a hollow tree draped over with a red cloth, which a drunken demon is drawing back. The saint is as calm as the sun-lit meadow at the edge of the woods next to the burning village, or that deer grazing on the roof of the ruin in the central panel. These are the serene corners of life, oblivious to tragedy that Auden spoke of in his great poem "Musée des Beaux Arts." Bosch, too, knew that truth. In *The Ascent to Calvary,* painted on the exterior of the right wing of the triptych, we see Christ collapsing under the weight of his cross while a small boy sitting on his father's shoulders is offering an apple to one of the men who has been mistreating our Lord. Again and again, Bosch insists, where there is evil, there's also innocence. Nobody ever saw them in such close proximity. That's what makes his paintings so terrifying.

Bosch's initial purpose was probably didactic. Temptation was an occasion to conjure up deadly sins and warn against them, but his imagination subverted the original impulse. I suspect he ended up enjoying the demonic beauty of his creations. Even more subversively, his habit of juxtaposing fantastic with realistic detail presents a deeply ambiguous view of creation and of humankind. An art that was supposed to be crystal clear to the faithful ended up by being an art rich in unsavory innuendoes. Every artist's imagination holds up a mirror to reality, both the outer and inner, but how those two realities will end up mingling in the reflection, the owner of the mirror may not even suspect. It's because the devils inside us are all poets, and so, luckily, are the angels.

Out on the street the weather had cleared, so we decided to walk until we found a place to have lunch. Lisbon is a large, bustling city of many hills with breathtaking views of the river Tejo that flows into the Atlantic a few miles beyond the harbor. What gives the city its distinctive character is the maze of old neighborhoods with narrow, cobbled streets, their houses covered with tiles and painted in bright colors. A blind man came around the corner and collided with me, giving me a good whack with his white cane. I wish I could say he resembled St. Anthony, but he did not. At the restaurant, a tall, lean, bearded waiter who served us dried linguica, grilled squid, and chicken and eel stew with shrimps, looked vaguely familiar, but we could not place him. We mentioned Vasco da Gama and a few other old navigators, and let it go at that. Late that night, I woke up, sat up in bed and saw the whole painting clearly and in its central panel the sharp profile of the "conjurer" in red with the beard of our waiter.

> *Again and again, Bosch insists, where there is evil, there's also innocence.*

CHOSEN PEOPLE

new fiction from Lisa Zeidne[r]

B.J. liked to pick up women at the Holocaust Memorial Museum. He liked to choose one, track her reactions to the cattle cars and heaped cadavers, and approach after the tour of the carnage, when she emerged, dazed and blinking, into the tastefully solemn Hall of Remembrance.

Imperfectly shaven in a leather jacket the supple brown of a chocolate Lab, B.J. could have been a resistance fighter. A five o'clock shadow of danger combined with courtliness: he could have been a count moonlighting as a pilot, because trying times demand trying measures. Shy behind wire rims, his eyes suggested that love was a brilliant weed that could sprout from the cement of the world's brutality.

This was not untrue. Even in the camps, people must have found crevices of time and space in which to have sex. To stay alive, you must hang on to desire.

B.J. liked Jewish women. Not that he had any burning desire to marry one again. Pale but not, generally, pasty, their long faces, framed by dark hair, were appealingly out-of-time, someone else's ancestral daguerreotypes. Some were jumpy as whippets, but he could enjoy that in controlled doses; could bolt one down like absinthe or Turkish coffee.

B.J. himself was a Southern boy—a Bobby Joe, in point of fact, though he'd never own up to that here, or to the equally trite initials. For Holocaust museum purposes, he was Rob. The accent was not a problem. An advantage, even. For the women he followed the trim asses of were not the ones who came to this shrine with a holy sense of belonging. On the contrary, he wanted the ones who *could not accept* a man like their fathers, but whose rage and ambivalence were so deep, so unruly, that they would never be so obvious as to date, say, a black bongo player with dreadlocks who plays for change in the subway. Rob is an *architect,* they could huff.

He was not even circumcised. Of course that would not generally be evident until later. Likewise, the women could not know, when informed of his profession, that he was a failed architect (was there, really, any other kind?) A low-level CADD operator, detailer of hideous, derivative, squat strip malls and office parks, whose workday offered little more outlet for creativity than your average data-entry clerk for a credit-reporting bureau. Despite the reality, "architect" as a profession still managed to sound dashing. Further it gave him and the women something to discuss, since everyone knew that the architecture of the Holocaust museum was supposed to be interesting.

B.J. did not tell the women how much he disliked the architecture, and not merely out of professional jealousy, this being the kind of project he himself would never enjoy, despite having dutifully learned to hash-sling phrases like "conceptual parti" in grad school. He loved bridges and arches, steel and brick, thought them luscious and noble; he resented the materials themselves being symbolically linked with the Third Reich. He even had a mental bumper sticker to sum up his objection to the unfair bad-reputation-by-association:

Stainless steel didn't kill Jews. Nazis did.

His ex-wife's brother—whom he still saw, since Mike was still his physician, and his friend—was the only person he had told about his use of the venue. Mike got "a kick" out of B.J. and considered it brilliantly subversive to hit on women in front of a portentously enlarged photo of Kristallnacht rather than, say, a curvy Matisse nude. B.J. did not find this praise condescending, since Mike was far more complicated than he seemed. He too had married outside his class and faith, suffering the scorn of his family. The men shared a conviction that miscegenation not only produced better and better-looking human beings, but was the very cornerstone of progress and civilization. Look at the English—their fine, refined race begot by wave after wave of invasion.

"You guys can't possibly believe that," B.J.'s ex-wife, Elaine, had scoffed, at the Thanksgiving dinner close to a decade ago when the topic had come up. "It's such kindergarten bullshit. You're actually proposing history as a nice-nice Rainbow Coalition, perfectly balanced and harmonious, like some Pepsi ad?"

"Not harmonious," Mike had shot back, "but definitely *vive la dif-*

ference. And there's scientific evidence for it, too. All those studies where they ask women to sniff the armpits of worn men's shirts, see who they want to screw. They like the B.O. most different from their own. The nose knows—the gene pool wants to vary up its act. Unless you're Amish."

"God, you're a dolt," Elaine had huffed. Mike was the little brother. He had not yet finished medical school. His brand-new girlfriend and wife-to-be, a placid, fine-boned WASP, had looked alarmed during this exchange; as soon as was polite, she'd left to busy herself in the kitchen. B.J. himself had played the impressionable newcomer at one point, the trembling hick right out of *The Rocky Horror Picture Show*, witnessing the brutality of the family's wit. Elaine had eventually remarried a nice, ambitious Jewish stock-market guy who served on the board of directors of many significant Manhattan cultural institutions, condescending to people like B.J. on a daily basis. When her first child was born, she'd begun to keep kosher, which had shocked B.J. deeply. The only explanation he could devise was that she needed an excuse to design a kitchen with many, many different cabinets and preparation areas, but Mike said that it was very common for people to discover their devout inner children when they became parents.

B.J. stood by what they'd said. One thing you must hand to sex: it is democratic. Aside from whips and chains, studs and black leather, or movies where Nazi soldiers snatch their snatch from the line of the doomed, sex, like death, is a great equalizer. An ass, grabbed, knows no race or place. Paradoxically, however, sex renders you more vulnerable to falling in love, and love returns you to the dangerous myth of individuality. The conviction that a life—say, your own—can matter in the great meat grinder of history. This is what B.J. contemplated as he watched footage of emaciated bodies being cleared away by bulldozer. Someone once wanted to kiss, solely, each one of those mouths. Each tongue, each tooth *connected*. To commit a sexual act in the face of death was therefore not sacrilege, but sanctimony.

"What we have tried to do," the architect was quoted as saying in *Progressive Architecture,* "is to construct symbolic forms that in some cases were very banal, ought to be banal, and in other cases are more abstract and open ended." No shit, Sherlock. *Banal* summed up neatly, for B.J., the museum's elevator. Once you surrender your timed pass to a uniformed guard, you take an identification card that "tells the story of a real person who lived during the Holocaust" and board a somber elevator—steel, of course—to deliver you to the exhibitions. People face forward and fold their hands before them, reverent as churchgoers, but their eyes are avid, awaiting the horrors above. When you are an American, confident that the worst thing likely to ever happen to you is to be trapped in an elevator for several hours with sweaty strangers, you take amusement-park rides, bungee-jump, watch disaster movies about airplanes or high-rises.

A pickpocket could work very efficiently in the Holocaust museum elevator. That would be amusingly craven. The elevator often made B.J. think of one of his nephew's Nintendo 64 games. "Yah-poo!" Super Mario exclaims as he jumps from platform to platform above quicksand, abysses.

Sometimes B.J. found her right there in the elevator. It wasn't appearance that drew him so much as movement. Something swift would twitch in her: a pang of pre-lunch hunger or need to look down at her new shoes. Exactly twice, women had already been taking his measure. (He had not lied to Mike about his small success rate at this enterprise, nor was it his fault that to Mike, still married, any ratio of call to response was impressive.) Those women were, not surprisingly, among the willing. Mandy, recovering from a breakup, sweetly timid, then immediately, skipping afterglow, accusatory. Like reliving his entire marriage in time-lapse. Ildiko, tourist from Budapest, zesty as Popeye. Generally B.J. did not gravitate toward tourists. Ideal as they'd be logistically (with, even, their own hotel rooms), B.J. could not be accused of wanting to carve the names of his conquests on a commemorative wall. He fully expected to marry again, and this certainly was more likely with someone he could meet for dinner by Metro than with Anna from Amsterdam. Still, he was ready to go where love led him.

Wasn't one of the Holocaust's lessons that you must be willing to leave your Picassos on the wall and bail? People deluded themselves that in the Jews' place they would have bravely boarded the ship at the first sign of trouble, but that is merely the safety of hindsight. There was no Vietnam Museum on the Washington Mall—too much ambiguity. Better to bemoan cartoon Nazis in their armbands.

Once you got off the elevator, the hallways were designed to chunnel you through the exhibitions, but here, as on the highway, people rudely passed. Most of the women who appealed to B.J. dawdled behind their companions if they had them, spending longer than usual on something less obvious than the Auschwitz room, where people can elbow each other to rubberneck at the crematoriums. They were in front of the huge photo of the fifteen thousand pounds of human hair (think of all the wigs, B.J. once heard someone note, that hair could have made for the women of Brooklyn's Orthodox community), or even poring over the guest register near the gift shop ("This really sucks, man," one teenager had written. "Love, Beavis and Butt-head").

The very young women, with their vacant expressions and low-riding jeans over cloddish shoes, did not much appeal to him. You couldn't blame them for not knowing the history of their grandparents' war, but B.J. felt himself way too jaded for the kind of dewy-eyed exploration a woman that young would demand. He was no Casanova; he brought to bed all of his dashed hopes; sex, he knew even as he felt himself flush from pleasure at a trim hip, pursed lip, or balletic walk, would disappoint him as had everything else, and this disappointment was not something Prozac could cure, though Mike had suggested it once, casually.

Only an idiot, B.J. believed, would *not* be depressed. Arms and clitorises were being chopped off all over the globe, in what was generously called the Third World but was really the Ninth or Tenth, by preteens with Uzis who made the Gestapo look like Cub Scouts—what exactly was that lesson the Holocaust was supposed to have taught us?—while in the home of the brave and the free, Commerce had triumphed so totally that even museums were voyeuristic entertainment centers. In all fairness, the architecture of the Third Reich was perfectly tasteful—an updating of the very neoclassicism that had inspired the Washington Mall. Whereas the "tasteful" Holocaust museum gave away, as party favors, passports of genuine Jews! *Please turn page at end of 4th floor,* the instructions offered, to help people get into the spirit! The whole country one gigantic shopping mall, B.J. himself a humble manservant.

That Saturday he had failed to engage a sultry, knock-kneed woman in the Hall of Remembrance. Her blue-black, frankly artificial hair was cropped close, like a camp inmate's or Mia Farrow's in *Rosemary's Baby*. She'd spent a long time in the Resistance section, one of B.J.'s favorite haunts, squinting at the pullquote about Irene Gut Opdyke, who saved eighteen people by playing mistress to a major in Tarnopol. At the end of the exhibitions B.J. zeroed in. But she would not even look at him, even though she was lost and impatient, in search of something. Her boyfriend, it turned out.

> "She'd spent a long time in the Resistance section, one of B.J.'s favorite haunts"

B.J. venomously witnessed their reunion kiss.

The museum had installed a container for recycling the identification cards, since it had become embarrassing to have the sad histories of dead Jews littering the grass outside as people left. B.J. watched now, mesmerized, as a black child of about ten removed the bubble gum from his mouth, smashed it between the pages of his passport, and gleefully dropped the passport in the recycling container. You were not even allowed to note, anymore, that a person was black.

"Charming," someone said, at his side, in an accent so close to his own that it had to be—Georgia? Tennessee? But tempered by college and—Manhattan? She was all in black. A trim, blondish, heavily freckled woman. "Just the spot where I'd take a kid. But hey, as we all know, slavery was much, much worse. 'Course *I'm* not allowed to say that, being a *plantation owner* and all. Guess what? Slavery isn't new. Ask the Greeks. The potato famine wasn't all that much fun either, and let me ask you: Do *you* know your ancestors' names? Can *you* trace your lineage right back to the king? Who has their own names, in this country? Smith? Taylor? I'm surprised, by the way, that you like her," and here she jerked her head toward the jet-black-haired woman. "Seems a little . . ." She stared at B.J., challenging.

"Come here often?" she asked.

He wondered how long she had been watching him. Had he actually been stalked? He had not noticed her at all, anywhere, which, given his vigilance, seemed impossible. The way she had just laid her political cards on the table to a stranger—it seemed bold enough to qualify as deranged, although her posture (arms folded, head tucked chinward) seemed guarded enough. What made her suspect he was a reasonable recipient for un-politically correct invective? Did he look, despite the Oliver Peoples specs and cool shoes, like a *good ole boy?*

"So what do you think?" he asked, making a sweep with his hands to indicate the room.

Her eyes registered surprise, which she choked off. She had not recognized him as a co-Confederate until he spoke. On what basis, then, had he been selected? Bachelorhood alone?

"Thought I just said," she answered. "I just want to make it known, however: *Mass murder is a bad thing.* I'm totally against it. Slavery, too. *Extremely* poor idea."

"Of the architecture, I mean."

She sighed. She drew his attention downward to the point of one of her ankle boots, which she now aligned, in a mildly parodic ballet position, with the grout joint on one of the triangular granite floor tiles. "Triangles," she said. "Mind you, I don't have anything *against* triangles. A nifty change from right angles. But is it supposed to *mean* something? Okay, a Jewish star—I understand it's pointy—but to have the edges look threatening, like ice picks: I don't get it. I mean . . . why?"

That was the moment when B.J. knew he could fall in love.

"Have you seen the famous sharp-edged building corner of Pei's addition to the National Gallery?" he asked.

She nodded. The nod might have meant she had, or had not. He went on.

"A thirty-degree angle in Tennessee marble. Technical feat, no boubt adout it. Everybody needs to come up and say, *Bet that was hard to do,* then stroke it, so the entire expensively produced and elegant joint is all worn down, turned black."

"Care to show me?" she asked.

B.J. realized that he was breathing hard, from the effort of having to evaluate her all at once rather than surreptitiously, in stages. She made a sweep like the one he'd done, about the room, to show her willingness to be inspected by Quality Control. But the erstwhile object of B.J.'s affection, with her tiny silver backpack and her galoot boyfriend, was ready to leave, taking a path that demanded their inserting themselves right between B.J. and this new woman. B.J. recognized, now, the error of his ways. Blue-hair suddenly seemed ridiculous, Olive Oyl-ish, clearly inferior to this woman with her pageboy, in her priestly black, who was "neat as a pin," as his mother would say, except for the random splatter art of the freckles.

B.J. was not particularly attracted to her. But that wasn't the point. Or rather, that was exactly the point. What do you know about people by how they look? We're all supposed to be enlightened enough to declare, *Nothing.* Phrenology not science at all. Red hair no more makes someone "fiery" than freckles make them "spunky." And yet. And yet. We all make our instantaneous judgments. He had been selected, here, on the basis of *something.* He wanted to trust her enough to see where things led.

He knew that his next gesture was important, and he didn't have long to invent it. He was thrilled to have to act with no facts. He looked at her gravely. He shifted position so that he could offer his arm. "I'll show you," he said. Wordlessly, with a wince of shyness, she took the arm with both of hers in a quaint way that seemed to require long white gloves.

B.J. had a flash of this encounter's ultimate position in the line of encounters he had enjoyed here. For this to be the Final Solution to his thus-far failed personal life, a life as blind and botched as history itself, shouldn't he and this woman find a handicapped bathroom somewhere, go at it? Any old dark semi-private alcove. A tour of the

> "But in love, small spaces are bowers. Secret gardens."

Holocaust museum made small spaces seem claustrophobic: the bunk beds at Auschwitz like the head-to-foot sardine layout of the galleys of slave ships; Anne Frank's minuscule apartment, shared with strangers, so she couldn't even find a private place to write small in her diary. But in love, small spaces are bowers. Secret gardens. Her hands around his arm were so thrilling that the fantasy he'd been mentally playing out, mentally bragging about later to Mike—which involved, for some reason, her having her period, them not caring—dissolved into a powerful feeling of *safety*.

They would come back here together always, he knew. A private ritual. Mike would be best man. He would take some flak in his family. For all B.J. knew, she would not like it much either. "Hey," he could imagine himself saying, "I *like* Mike."

Her name, he was about to learn, was Rebecca, and she was one of a handful of Jews to grow up in North Carolina, where her father was: *an architect*. An architect who had been actively involved with the civil-rights movement in the fifties and was now fixated on his hatred of the Nation of Islam, which had actually accused his ancestors of perpetrating the slave trade. The sundry straggling colonial Jews with capital to invest, rather than the Portuguese! When it came time for B.J. to tell Rebecca that he was an architect, her response would be, "I'm so sorry for you." When he tried out the line, *Funny, you don't look Jewish,* she'd laugh. Her mother was a Georgia belle, awakened by love into political conscience. Her maternal grandfather and B.J.'s grandfather (either of his would have done, but only one was alive) could sit together at the wedding, emboldened by champagne to admit to each other that they're not entirely sure the Holocaust ever happened. This museum was unlikely to change their minds: they were not so old and naïve as to not know that photographs could be rigged. Even old black-and-white footage.

"Wait," Rebecca said. They had not moved, B.J. realized, from the recycling container. It had taken only a second for him to spin out

Subscribe now and save 50% off the single copy price.

Use this card to enter your own subscription or give Tin House to a friend.

TIN HOUSE
"With a publisher like Win McCormack, how can you lose?" *www.salon.com - May 1999.*

CHARTER OFFER- SAVE 50%

Yes! Enter my Charter Subscription to TIN HOUSE at the incredibly low charter rate of $19.95 for one year (four issues).

☐ Payment enclosed   ☐ Please bill me

Name

Address

City   State   Zip

B9902A

TIN HOUSE
"...this little book may well represent the future of literary magazines." *The Village Voice - June 1999*

GIVE THE PERFECT GIFT. SAVE 50%

Yes! I want to give one year of TIN HOUSE (4 issues) for only $19.95. That's 50% off the newsstand cost.

Please send TIN HOUSE to:

Name

Address

City   State   Zip

Bill me:

Name

Address

City   State   Zip

B9902B

Priority Order Form

BUSINESS REPLY MAIL
FIRST-CLASS MAIL PERMIT NO 35 LANGHORNE PA

POSTAGE WILL BE PAID BY ADDRESSEE

P. O. Box 10500
Portland, OR 97296-0500

NO POSTAGE
NECESSARY
IF MAILED
IN THE
UNITED STATES

ENJOY HOME DELIVERY OF TIN HOUSE USE THE CARDS TO SUBSCRIBE TODAY.

Priority Order Form

BUSINESS REPLY MAIL
FIRST-CLASS MAIL PERMIT NO 35 LANGHORNE PA

POSTAGE WILL BE PAID BY ADDRESSEE

P. O. Box 10500
Portland, OR 97296-0500

NO POSTAGE
NECESSARY
IF MAILED
IN THE
UNITED STATES

SUBSCRIBE AND SAVE 50% WITH THIS CHARTER OFFER

this whole premonition of their joint destiny—their lives flashing before his eyes.

"Shall we?" Rebecca asked.

They found their identification cards, in unison checked the last pages. Both his and her tour guides to the museum had survived their separate death camps, emigrated to the United States in 1947. B.J. pointed out that their twosome might have met on the ship. She retilted her chin in a way that seemed to suggest a lot, most of it contradictory: that this meeting was indeed fated, as meant-to-be as if it had happened on Ellis Island; that she might not stick around for more than lunch. They dropped the identification cards in the container for reincarnation and once more Rebecca took his arm.

B.J. had this thought as her hand landed. *She's the kind of woman who will cry when she comes.* Never at the standard sentimental things, though. Never at dead heroes in movies. For that second he enjoyed the absolute conviction of the premonition, as strong as his belief that they would marry: that her strong shudders would so deeply move her, she would weep. He was wrong, actually, but by the time he discovered he was wrong, it would no longer matter.

On the way out, Rebecca did something that made B.J. so fond of her it caused him a sharp pain in his gut. As they walked past a brushed stainless steel railing, she had to release one of her arms to touch it. As a boy B.J. had stroked everything he passed on the walk home from school, drawn to each new texture, so that his hands and nails were always filthy, cut, and splintered. Maybe all boys did this. The ones who didn't stop became architects. His ex-wife had berated him about just this habit: *Stop touching things!* But the architect's daughter put down just the pads of her fingers on the steel, as if blessing it, or savoring the material's coolness.

"Pretty," she said.

PILGRIMAGE

Nothing is Lost or Found: Desperately Seeking Jane and Paul Bowles

LYNNE TILLMAN

Anarchic, idiosyncratic, inscrutable—these words only begin to describe the ineffable literary couple.

I once read: "All journeys have destinations of which the traveler is unaware." The beginnings of journeys and narratives can be as surprising as their secret destinations. They can start as mysteriously as they end, they can start before one thinks. I was living in Amsterdam in 1972 when I was given a Valentine's Day gift, an anthology entitled *Americans Abroad*. It had been published in The Hague in 1932, in English, and was an out-of-print and rare book. It included well-known American expatriate writers—Stein, Pound, Eliot—less well-known ones—Harry and Caresse Crosby—and many unknowns. The unknowns dominated, the way they usually do. Immediately, I wanted to edit a new one, to represent American writers now, or then. Some months later, I was introduced to an editor who had a novelty imprint at a large Dutch publishing house. He liked the idea. He also liked enormously obese women and had posters of them, nude, hidden in his office. After he got to know me a little, he showed them to me. I remember this very well and the fact that on signing the contract he paid me an advance of fifteen hundred guilders.

I think 1971 was the year I read Paul Bowles's *The Sheltering Sky* and Jane Bowles's *Two Serious Ladies*. I knew that Jane Bowles was ill, in a Spanish hospital, unable to speak her name, and I also knew that Paul Bowles was installed in Tangier and had been since the 1940s. To me, he was the preeminent American abroad (the term is aptly dated), and I was determined to have him in the book.

Writing a letter to Paul Bowles was alarming, and I worked on it for a week. After deliberating, in a circuitous and paranoid way, I decided not to reveal that I was female. It was the era of William Burroughs's vicious or satiric retort to feminism, *The Job*. Burroughs and Bowles were friends; I considered, in a convoluted way, that even though Paul Bowles was married to Jane Bowles, if he was in any way like some of his friends, or affected by their mean-spiritedness, he might now hate women and not want to be in a book edited by one. This might not be true at all—and if it were, why would I want him in the book? But I was in Amsterdam, smoking hash. I concocted a sexless letter, signed it Lynne Merrill Tillman (Lynne is also a man's name; Merrill is my mother's maiden name) and mailed it.

Bowles quickly replied that he'd be happy to be in the anthology. I'd asked for original material; he wrote that he'd send me some, and did. After another letter or two—I've kept all of his letters—I received one in which he inquired if I were a man or a woman, and how he should address me— Miss, Mrs. or Mr.? Otherwise he was "obliged to use Dear Lynne Merrill Tillman." I wrote that I was female, in a letter I hope is lost, and he thanked me in his next letter for setting him straight.

The anthology's publication date kept being postponed, and everything Bowles had given me appeared elsewhere. Finally he wrote that he had no more new or unpublished work to contribute except some poems he'd written in the late 1920s or early 1930s, and, he said, they weren't

Paul Bowles in Tangier, 1987, by Lynne Tillman

very good. I wrote that they'd be included even if they weren't very good, because I had to have him in the book. But, I asked, didn't he have anything else, maybe some letters he'd written?

Bowles sent two letters he wrote his mother when he first went to Europe in 1931 with composer Aaron Copland. One told the hilariously anxious tale of his and Copland's nearly missing a boat from Spain to Morocco. The other was written from the south of France, where he was visiting Gertrude Stein and Alice B. Toklas for the first time. I was overwhelmed by my good luck.

Encouraged by our friendly, frequent correspondence—it was now 1976 or 1977 and I was in New York—I asked him for some writing from Jane Bowles. Requesting her work was even harder than asking for his. She was dying when I began the project, and I didn't feel comfortable asking him for her work then or right after she'd died. I didn't want Paul to feel taken advantage of. I thought her death must have been so painful for him that even mentioning her name would upset him. I hesitated a long time. I didn't appreciate then that people usually don't want the people they love to be forgotten. Jane Bowles is often and usually forgotten.

I wanted her desperately. Her novel, *Two Serious Ladies*, was a revelation—a work of genius, unique, subversive. These terms are overused, and usually misused, but are true of this audacious, brilliantly written novel, this masquerade, comedy, tragedy, with its anarchic, singular views of sexuality, marriage, femininity, masculinity, American culture, exoticism. Jane Bowles ignored the worn lines between conscious and unconscious life; she beggared the realist novel with writing indifferent to prosaic notions of reality. Her dialogue is the most particular and idiosyncratic in American literature, as peculiar and condensed as speech in jokes and dreams. I loved and respected Paul Bowles's *The Sheltering Sky*, "He of the Assembly," and "Pages from Cold Point." But Jane Bowles's novel shifted the ground for me— she made the world of writing move. Move over and sigh.

Paul Bowles sent two fragments from a notebook of hers, just a few paragraphs. I was thrilled. With the Bowleses' contributions, I thought, the anthology had a reason to exist. But it was abandoned by its first publisher (the novelty imprint was dissolved) and then again, in about 1980, by its second, a friend who was a small press publisher. One of Jane Bowles's paragraphs was later quoted in Millicent Dillon's excellent biography of her, *A Little Original Sin*, but the other— about getting married and loneliness—has still not been published. Of it Paul Bowles wrote, "I find it a complete mystery, myself."

Our correspondence continued. We wrote about domestic life—collapsing roofs—and dreams we had. He typed his letters on white, crinkly airmail paper. His signature, in black pen, was neat and without any flourishes. I have a couple of letters on green airmail paper written entirely in his legible hand. In one he wrote: "Place seems to have become unimportant."

The anthology receded from consciousness, and I threw myself into writing and co-directing an independent feature film called *Committed*. It was released in 1984, and I was, too, to finish writing *Haunted Houses*, my first novel, which was published in 1987. On its back cover was a quote from the late Kathy Acker that began: "Lynne Tillman, daughter of Jane Bowles." Jane Bowles never had any children, and it didn't occur to me that when the book came out people would think Jane Bowles was my mother. But an acquaintance stopped me on St. Marks Place and said, "I thought your mother was in Florida." One reviewer wrote that "the author mentioned her mother, Jane Bowles," in the novel, and it was a problem. Acker plagiarized texts, wrote characters who invented multiple identities, invoked "her" mother and father, and no one knew what was fact or fiction. It was ironically appropriate that she inadvertently bestowed a legend upon me, a fictitious literary genealogy. On bad days I imagined it was the best thing about me.

I sent my novel to Paul Bowles, hoping he wouldn't be bothered by the quotation about Jane Bowles and me. He read the book, which was very generous of him, more generous than I recognized then. He even liked it. He said it reminded him of a Russian novel, because he confused the protagonists. He didn't mention the quote, and this lack—and the existence of the quote itself—became another layer in the strange and stealthy background of my journey to him. Even his allusion to a Russian novel seemed part of the confusion of character and characters that preceded me and ensued when I finally arrived in Tangier in August 1987.

I wanted to talk with Bowles in person, because I hoped to make a film of *Two Serious Ladies*. It would be my homage to Jane Bowles, and maybe it would bring attention to her work. I could picture the book as a film, its bizarre scenes happily haunted by the ghost of director Preston Sturges, its eccentric dialogue delivered by actors like Lily Tomlin (she'd play Miss Goering, one of the two serious ladies). Bowles thought the film rights had been sold years ago, but he couldn't remember to whom. I found the person I was told was Jane Bowles's agent, who would presumably know. And so starts a terrible story, one I can tell in expurgated form only, to protect others and also myself from further misunderstanding and even the law.

The agent knew nothing about the rights and actually didn't have them, yet involved me in discussions over four months about my buying them. In my first visit I explained that it would be a very low-budget film, and in the last the agent announced: I've taken a look at the story, and it is a little longer than I thought it was. Actually, it's longer than her other stories. So I'll have to ask you for one hundred thousand dollars. Crushed, I left the office.

I was informed by my agent, after she studied the novel's copyright notice, that the book might be in the public domain. I asked the Library of Congress to do a copyright check, in fact three, and each time the book turned up in the public domain. Still unconvinced, I traveled to Washington, D.C., to that great house of copyrights, where I was brought to a room the size of a football field and shown the file cabinet that held the card for Jane Bowles's only novel. The copyright had not been renewed by her publisher in 1973—the year she died. They'd forgotten. The book was like Shakespeare, the library told me.

I wrote the script and, with the Library's authorization, received two grants to make the movie. I was slowly moving forward when one day I received a call from a lawyer who told me his client owned the rights, that the book was not in the public domain in Europe, and that they would stop me from showing the film. Confused, I hired a lawyer, and the sorry story continued.

I met Buffie Johnson, a painter friend of the Bowleses, and visited her in her apartment in SoHo. She offered to introduce me to Paul in Tangier, where she summered. Though I didn't need an introduction—everyone drops in on him in the afternoon and we'd been corresponding for years—I accepted her offer gratefully, eagerly. Buffie had had an affair with Jane Bowles in the 1940s. Jane dropped her, she said, because Jane liked older women, and she and Jane were the same age. Buffie told me that in those days homosexuals married each other and that Jewish people, like Jane, kept their religion quiet. After I commented that Mrs. Copperfield, in *Two Serious Ladies,* could have been code for Mrs. Goldberg, Buffie continued, in a lower register, that before the war everyone was a little anti-Semitic.

A disturbing event happened just weeks before I left for Tangier. I received a copy of a letter Jane Bowles's agent had sent Paul Bowles. It warned of my imminent arrival, that I was trying to steal Jane Bowles's work, that I was, in short, a thoroughly bad character. The letter was meant to deter me, I suppose. But how did the agent know I was going to Tangier? What network was I in, who had betrayed me? All along I'd been writing to Bowles about my dealings with the agent and the Library of Congress, detailing my mostly futile attempts at getting to the bottom of things, where truth supposedly resides. I felt I had nothing to hide. Obviously, I was naïve. If I make any money from the film, I wrote him, I'd be happy to give you half. He had not profited from the recent sale of the rights, and the idea that I was in this for the money was grotesquely amusing.

The situation had become byzantine. Everything connected closely to Paul Bowles, I would discover, was and wouldn't be a surprise to him. He knew much worse characters, perhaps, than I could ever be or aspire to—Cherifa, for instance, Jane's Moroccan lover. She was rumored to have poisoned Jane. I didn't believe this and hoped Paul Bowles didn't, either, just as I hoped he wouldn't believe I was the mercenary, flawed character the agent described.

David Hofstra, a musician and the man I live with, accompanied me to Tangier. We took a room in the famous—now defunct—Hotel Ville de France. Matisse had stayed there and painted the view out of his hotel window. David and I went immediately to see Buffie. She was waiting for us in the apartment Jane Bowles had lived in years before, just above Paul's. (The Bowleses kept separate apartments.) Then, like a security guard, Buffie escorted us to Paul's apartment, and walking down the stairs, my breathing became stuck in me or suspended. My life was about to change or stay shockingly the same.

We knocked, the door opened, we entered and were introduced to Bowles. He was, he said, about to go to the beach. Would we come back tomorrow afternoon? I handed him the script, we left and I breathed. I didn't know what he was wearing or even what he looked like. If I had an image of him, it wasn't contested by the reality of seeing him. I hadn't seen him. He might be running away from me, I thought, but when he was there the next day, I decided he wasn't. Maybe just stalling for time. (Later I was told that days before, another writer had rushed from London to Tangier, to advise him not to sell the rights. But did he have them to sell?)

He liked the script, Bowles told me; it was faithful to the book. But, he said firmly, I can't help you. My lawyer had asked the other lawyer for evidence, a document authenticating ownership of the rights. None was ever produced. My lawyer believed Paul Bowles could exercise his rights as the inheritor of Jane Bowles's estate, if he wanted. Yet what Bowles had once written me spun another cautionary literary tale. A publisher had gone to Spain to see Jane in the hospital. The publisher asked Paul to leave the hospital room, so he could be alone with her, and when the publisher emerged, he held a piece of paper in his hand. The publisher had gotten Jane to sign something, when she didn't know what she was signing. On this scrap of paper, the film rights to the book rested. That was the story. Bowles never contested the publisher's claim. He lived in Tangier, it was explained to me, precisely because he didn't want to become involved in ordinary and tawdry matters like fights over rights.

Now, a little numb or stunned, with the film out of the way, or dead, I could try to have a good time. There I was, sitting with Paul Bowles in his darkened living room, drinking tea served by the taciturn Mohammed Mrabet, Bowles's companion. I'd read Mrabet's stories, which Bowles had taped and written down. They were published in Mrabet's name, but bore the mark of Bowles's spare, elegant style. Mrabet, I found out later, had once asserted that Bowles was merely his typist.

I greedily listened to Bowles's stories about Jane and himself. In 1943, during the war, when Jane was living in New England with her lover, Helvetia, he told us, he was in Mexico. He was still writing music and needed one of his instruments—a drum. But he couldn't remember where it was. He wrote Jane and asked if it was in Staten Island, or with her in New England, or in their apartment in New York? There was some urgency to his request, and Jane Bowles sent a telegram in return: Drum not in basement, not on Staten Island, not in New York. Drum can't be found. The day after, the doorbell rang at Jane's residence. It was the FBI.

FBI: Your husband was in Morocco in the spring of 1942?
Jane: Yes.
FBI: And in South America in the fall of that year?
Jane: Yes.
FBI: He's in Mexico now?
Jane: Yes.
FBI: Why does he travel so much?
Jane: I guess he's restless.

By now Helvetia, at Jane's request, was burning some of their papers in the fireplace, though it was the summer. But after questioning her a little longer, the FBI was mollified. It turned out that there was a colonel in the army named Drum, and her telegram had been intercepted—all telegrams were read during the war. The FBI thought they might have uncovered an underground group plotting to assassinate Colonel Drum.

In Bowles's darkened living room, above the couch, was a single bookshelf. On it were all of Jane Bowles's books, all the editions, in all the languages into which they'd been translated. The shelf was a shrine to her, and I felt her presence in his life and in the room through her books. I plucked up the courage to question him about her novel. Why had Jane Bowles named one of the serious ladies Miss Goering? Bowles looked amused and said: That was Jane's little joke.

I remember saying, tentatively: I think I've got an idea for another novel. Bowles nonchalantly said, I haven't had an idea in twenty years.

We intended to take him to dinner but didn't. We visited him three times and met him on the street once. We took photographs of him alone, with Buffie, and of Buffie alone. David took some of me and them. Bowles didn't like being photographed and turned wooden. I made him laugh in one and that shot came out blurred. It was too bad. He looked very handsome laughing.

Paul Bowles never mentioned Kathy Acker's quote. I shouldn't have been surprised. Some years before I'd mailed him a story in which I'd quoted a line from his autobiography, *Without Stopping*. He wrote a long letter about it and questioned me on an interesting point of grammar. He never mentioned my tribute to him. His reserve, discretion, or secretiveness was impressive, intimidating, or disturbing.

It's unsettling and strange rendering this account and calling up faulty memory to describe my pilgrimage, if that's what it was, to him and the spirit of Jane Bowles. I was as close to her as I'd ever be. Her presence was almost palpable—I wanted her to be there—and always evanescent, like life itself. Even stranger was the sensation I had when I was with Paul. Sometimes I felt I was his daughter, as if that quote had created a symbolic link between us, even a blood tie, in an extraordinary demonstration of the power of fiction. It was a feeling, too, that I got, after my father died, around older men I liked who were difficult to know, the way my father was. I admired Bowles' writing, its inscrutability, lack of apology and explanation, its dark humor, reserve, mystery. He had all of this, too. I didn't know him, I liked him, I didn't know what he thought of me. We laughed together, and I can like or feel familiar around anyone who's funny.

I gave up the film, returned one of the grants, was allowed to keep the other and use it toward writing the novel I'd mentioned to Bowles. It was called *Motion Sickness*, which now seems an appropriate title for the experience of writing this weird history of failure and desire. *Two Serious Ladies* has still not been made into a film.

After visiting Bowles, I began my letters "Dear Paul B." I sent him and Buffie copies of the photographs we'd taken, and he wrote a postcard thanking me. It ended, "Your visit to Tangier was very short, unfortunately. Another time, perhaps?" I haven't returned, but I did fly to Atlanta in 1995 to visit him when he came to the States for an operation. It was his first visit since 1968. I also saw him briefly at Lincoln Center for a concert of his music. These last years he's been ill and doesn't answer most letters. I treasure the ones I have.

— August 1999

· · · · · · ·

Paul Bowles died on November 18, 1999, at the age of 88.

NEW FICTION FROM

Mailman's House

The room where Mailman's wife used to sleep is now the mail room. It's a small corner bedroom with two narrow windows. Under one window is a five-foot collapsible buffet table with a fake wood-grain finish, on which has been placed a single-coil hot plate and teakettle, a reading lamp, a variety of liquid adhesives, pens and pencils, envelopes and stationery. Against the wall opposite this table are stacks of stolen milk crates (Mailman scavenged these one night from the loading dock of the dairy and secreted them away in his mail truck, which was and is above suspicion in the context of such missions) filled with mail, his own mail of many years. Not all of it, not the unsolicited catalogs and flyers and leaflets addressed to Resident or with carrier-route sorting instructions printed by computer, only his own personal mail, letters and postcards, and all business transactions carried on through the mail, which is Mailman's preferred method of conducting his affairs. The crates are blue with metal supports and reach, in some stacks, to the ceiling. They are clearly marked by year, beginning with 1944, when Mailman received his first piece of mail, a handwritten letter from Europe, where his father had gone to fight the war.

MAILMAN

J. ROBERT LENNON

Behind the door is a photocopier, bought for a song at a federal government office auction twelve years before. He is fully capable of servicing it himself, and did so regularly until about five years ago, by which time he had replaced or improved practically every part, and it has run without significant difficulty every day since. The wall opposite the door is hidden by a row of four-drawer filing cabinets, all black, salvaged from the P.O. in 1987, when they were replaced for reasons still unclear. They contain photocopies of personal and business communications, descriptions of the contents of packages, and other miscellany that Mailman took certain liberties with before delivering it to its proper destination.

Mailman is aware of the import of the word *destination*. It refers to the place all mail in his charge must reach on the day he picks it up from the P.O. What happens to it in the interim is nobody's business but his own.

On the floor, with a narrow strip of carpet surrounding it on all sides, is the thin mattress Mailman occasionally sleeps on when, after hours of close work in the mail room, he is too weary to retire to his bedroom proper, formerly the bedroom he shared with his wife before she made what is now the mail room her bedroom.

Mailman's Route

At eight-thirty every morning Mailman arrives at the P.O. in his truck to pick up the day's mail. Over the years, this mail has changed in character, from the relatively light and uniformly sized to the pointlessly bulky. It has also greatly increased in volume. This mail is sorted numerically by street address and filed into translucent white plastic trays for his convenience. When the mail is loaded onto the truck, Mailman drives to his house, pulls into the alley behind it, presses the green button on a gray garage-door control he keeps in the truck, and pulls into his garage. It is unusual for anyone to see him do this. Across the alley from the garage is a ten-foot hedge, grown by Mailman's neighbor to create a physical and psychological barrier between himself and Mailman. This is fine by Mailman. Once in the garage, Mailman turns on the overhead light and unloads the mail onto a pair of buffet tables identical to the one in the mail room and sorts through it for things that look interesting. Mostly he selects from ongoing correspondences of either a business or private nature, or new combinations of sender and addressee that seem promising. Once he makes these selections he places them in a briefcase and carries the briefcase across the yard and into the house. He sets the briefcase on the floor of the mail room, sits down at his chair, turns on the hot plate and, while waiting for the kettle to boil, examines the day's interceptions.

An uninitiated observer would be surprised at the recklessness with which postal customers seal their letters. Many people are satisfied with only a cursory lick at the center of the adhesive strip, making Mailman's invasion almost insultingly easy. Businesses often fail to seal their mail at all, by either oversight or apathy. Some people simply tuck the flap into the envelope. On the other hand, there are those who seal with great care, making sure every last inch of adhesive has been moistened and affixed to the envelope's bare lower lip, and it is these senders who most interest Mailman, for it is a great challenge to overcome their fortifications and, generally speaking, of greater interest to read what they have so carefully concealed.

When the kettle is aboil, Mailman steams open the mail. It is important not to apply steam excessively, else the envelope will be permanently wrinkled. Only the necessary amount of steam must be employed, and the flap raised without haste, to prevent damage. Most flaps yield with little effort. Others are trickier, made with quality adhesive in generous amounts, and these require great care, and may demand a reapplication of adhesive when sealed. Very seldom does Mailman have trouble resealing mail. If he does, he can usually make the best of things, with his years of experience and diverse collection of tools and substances.

Rarely, a piece of mail must be sacrificed.

When the mail is opened, Mailman photocopies its contents. He does not read it at this point. The mail, after all, must be delivered. He then replaces the mail inside its envelopes and re-sorts it. He is careful to put the contents in the right envelopes. In the years before his method was perfected, he made mistakes. These went unpunished but not undetected. Postal customers smelled a rat. Not long afterward, Mailman was able to remove himself from danger by securing a new route, the one he has now. This route covers his own neighborhood.

Mailman delivers his own mail.

Once the mail is sealed and re-sorted, Mailman takes to the streets. His route circles past his own house several times, so that he does not need to bring his truck. Instead he pushes a two-wheeled cart with generous blue-gray pouches. The Northwest Quadrant is first, then the Northeast, the Southeast, the Southwest. With each loop he picks up more mail. The occasional large package waits until midafternoon.

Mailman's route has certain pitfalls.

Apartment buildings, with their old-fashioned racks of mailboxes that stick. Customers whose boxes remain untouched for weeks, stuffed with mail. Children who never seem to be in school, who follow his truck and demand rubber bands.

Dogs.

Mailman's wife lives in the Southwest Quadrant. A sign on the mailbox reads:

Dr. and Mrs. Francis Payne
414 West Longstreth

Mailman suspects the sign, which is new, was put there for his benefit.

He made mistakes. These went unpunished but not undetected. Postal customers smelled a rat.

Mailman's Hangout

Unless inconvenient circumstances prevail, Mailman's route is finished by four in the afternoon. At this time, Mailman parks his truck at the corner nearest the coffee shop, where the curb was painted yellow, but that was some time ago and the paint has since partially worn away. At any rate he has never been issued a parking ticket. Those who depend on mail, which is everyone, allow carriers certain privileges, the flouting of arbitrary civic regulation among them.

The coffee shop has been here four years, having replaced the grossly misnamed Yarn Barn (this particular retail space is part of a two-story brick storefront row), which itself replaced the Coal Miner's Bar, which had stood on this spot since time immemorial. Mailman admits to loving the coffee shop, he thinks it's wonderful, with its brick walls and archways and stained floorboards and the lovely smell of freshly brewed espresso and the mechanized slurp of steaming milk, but he refuses to utter its proper name, which is too cute by half for a place of such dignity, and will only call it the coffee shop. When he enters he heads straight for his favorite table, right next to the condiment shelves, where every customer who orders coffee, which is virtually everyone, must pass. In the event that this table is occupied he has a second choice, and if it too proves occupied he returns to the truck and drives home and makes his own, admittedly inferior, coffee, which he drinks in a barely controlled fit of rage, and on a good day he spills not a drop.

But on this day, as on most, his table is empty, and he claims it by tossing his wristwatch onto it, then goes to the coffee urns, reaches around and under the counter for a mug, and fills it with coffee. He then drops five quarters into the refill jar, four for the coffee and one for the refill he plans to drink. This is not the standard way of ordering coffee, but Mailman sees no reason to wait in line for something he knows perfectly well how to get himself. New clerks occasionally give him dirty looks until they learn.

He drinks it black. He drinks it as slowly as its fleeting warmth allows. He watches his postal customers walk in and out of the coffee shop, for the coffee shop is on his route, and these are the people whose mail he opens.

A woman named Rachel walks in holding a baby in a sling. The baby's name is Brittany and she was six pounds thirteen ounces at birth, and the baby's father is not Rachel's husband, which the husband does not know because the real father looks comfortingly similar to the husband, or at least was represented as such by Rachel in a letter to her sister MaryJane. MaryJane recently tried shaving her bikini line with her boyfriend's electric razor but didn't know how to operate it, and now she has brilliant red welts on her lower belly and thighs and can't wear a swimsuit, and out of embarrassment (for he is sure to mock her mercilessly and possibly hit her) has been begging off sexual intercourse with the boyfriend by complaining of unusually profuse menstrual flow, which disgusts him. To a high-school friend who now lives in Chicago, Rachel writes that even though she loves her sister, bless her soul, she thinks MaryJane is kind of a slut, and in fact used to spy on her when she, Rachel, was twelve and MaryJane was sixteen and had boys, or sometimes men, in bed with her on Saturday afternoons with both parents working out back in the garden. In fact, reports Rachel, it's how I learned about sex and consequently got myself into this mess, so like I should talk!

Mailman thinks she won't order coffee, because she "went off" coffee when she got pregnant and hasn't gone back on, as far as he's read. And in fact she orders iced tea and a corn muffin.

Mailman's Route

He is wondering if maybe Jenny Vandermeer will be in today, and sure enough here she comes. She lives in the Grape Street apartment complex with the mailbox doors that stick. He met her delivering a package once. The package was from her parents and he asked, having noted the return address, if she was from Grosse Pointe, Michigan, because (he lied) he in fact was from Grosse Pointe but hadn't been there in many years, and did she know (first thing off the top of his head) the Humanists?

Humanists? she asked, both hands on the package despite his hands on the other side not yet having let go.

Ronald and Patty Humanist, he said, yes, isn't that a funny name?

No, she didn't know them and she got back to Michigan every once in a while but mostly she and her folks communicated through the mail and could she have the package now please? He regretted as he gave it to her not having opened it first.

Now she orders a latte and a scone and smiles in recognition of him while she adds sugar to the latte, and when she leans toward him for a napkin her hair sweeps over her shoulder and sends a fresh, appley scent in his direction, and he inhales perhaps a little too loudly and she looks up as if to say Hmm? Did you say something?

Mailman grins and then searches the depths of his coffee, which he has allowed to get too cold. Jenny sits alone at a distant table and pulls out a thin paperback.

She has: a membership to a compact-disc club, a taste for expensive clothing, friends in Canada, no magazine subscriptions, low monthly telephone bills, and a monumental amount of credit-card debt.

She has been corresponding with an older man (he is forty-two, fifteen years younger than Mailman, but Mailman sees himself as still rather handsome, particularly in his postal uniform, and in good physical shape) with whom she was once in a relationship that had a con-

> When she leans toward him for a napkin her hair sweeps over her shoulder and sends a fresh, appley scent in his direction, and he inhales perhaps a little too loudly

siderable sexual element to it. This man, whose name is Mark, is a professor of some kind at Yale University and has a knack for description, particularly of Jenny's body and the things he once did to it and missed doing or longed to do at some future date. Jenny wrote:

I'd be lying if I said I didn't miss you, and though our union was satisfying sexually, I wonder if what I really need right now is some other kind of stimulation that doesn't come with so many strings attached.

Which, in Mailman's opinion, a lot of people might say but nobody ever really means, and he figures that Jenny is on some level pining away for this older fellow and that perhaps an older fellow with fewer commitment-related needs could suffice.

Mailman is still recovering from recent weeks away from his route, as correspondences continued in his absence and he has been forced to catch up on his customers' dizzying carnival of private-life events. The truth is, Mailman quit his job with the U.S. Postal Service. Some time ago Mailman's wife, visiting his house to retrieve a pair of hedge clippers of Dr. Payne's that she had (against her better judgment, she said) lent Mailman, was taken aback by the condition her former home had fallen into and seriously suggested to Mailman that he take some time off from delivering mail. She told Mailman outright that she thought he might be going mad, and said that he should give himself a break to sort out his various issues. Mailman took umbrage at this suggestion, but as he hadn't slept in several weeks determined privately that his wife could be right, so he spent several depressing afternoons discussing his problems with a psychologist employed by the P.O. to quell its employees' feelings of anxiety and hostility. The psychologist recommended a major change for Mailman, and Mailman agreed to take a leave of absence. However, Mailman became embroiled in an argument with his supervisor over the terms of his absence and quit outright, then applied and was accepted to join the efforts of the Peace Corps in the newly liberated nation of Belarus.

He was to help the citizens of a small town build a bridge over a sluggish, filthy river, to encourage commerce between the town's two halves. The effort was led by a Peace Corps official and two entrepreneurs from the Belarussian town, but quickly it became clear that the official resented the inexpert assistance of the entrepreneurs, and the entrepreneurs, whom Mailman had assumed were acting in the interests of the entire town, turned out simply to own a tavern on the crummy side of the river, and were the only people in the town who saw any pressing need to install a bridge. Furthermore, the town was heavily polluted by local factories, the electricity went out several times a week, and mail service was unreliable. Mail carriers drank openly from greasy bottles as they drove the rusted-out unmarked cars that served as delivery vehicles, and none of the people on his old route Mailman had sent postcards to the day he arrived had bothered to write back. It was not long before Mailman quit and returned to the United States, and within a few weeks he had his old job again. His replacement, a young man just out of junior college, was thought to be too slow and was promptly fired, and Mailman begged his supervisor for forgiveness, which he was granted, along with his route.

Mailman has slept soundly ever since.

Mailman's Wife

Mailman was never really well suited for marriage, and the irony that this fact is the only thing he believes he learned from his twenty-year marriage does not escape him. Mailman met his wife in a city very far from here, at a time when he never imagined himself delivering mail for a living. In fact, he was in graduate school, studying mathematics, and intended to become a mathematics professor. He was in his next-to-last semester of study when he had what he now recognizes as a nervous breakdown. While working out a routine problem in fluid dynamics, Mailman got off on a sort of tangent, and from there got off on still more tangents, until, many days later, he had developed a mathematical theory uniting all sciences, which explained the creation of the universe and its eventual destruction, and pretty much everything in between, including the rise of life on earth, the evolution of human intelligence and its products, sociological, economic, and artistic; and the quantum basis for love and war. He showed the pages of equations and diagrams to his supervisors, and when they failed to understand what he had done he brought the pages to the department of physics and the department of astronomy. Recalling this episode today, it does not surprise him that he and his equations came to rest at last at the university health center, where, over a two-week period of recuperation, he met and wooed a young and inexperienced nurse. Moved by his passionate and tragic story, she agreed to keep seeing him when he was feeling better, and it was not long before she had gotten engaged to him.

That summer he took the civil-service exam and began delivering mail on a part-time basis.

It took another ten years for Mailman to realize that mail delivery was all he would ever do, though much later, during the series of arguments leading up to divorce, Mailman's wife would claim that it only took her about six months.

Mailman's wife did not mind being married to a mail carrier. In fact, she preferred that Mailman have a steady government job, instead of remaining lashed to the treacherous sys-

Strictly speaking, Mailman's wife is no longer Mailman's wife.

tem of academic tenure. Furthermore, carrying mail kept Mailman fit, which appealed to her strong feelings about bodily well-being, and also served as a physical outlet for his anxieties and aggressions, which had proved quite considerable. Even so, it was not unusual for Mailman to smash some fragile something or kick a hole in a door or wall of the house they had bought in this small mountain town. She might have put up with all this had he kept his neuroses to himself, his endless preoccupations and prejudices and rituals and tics and rants and boycotts and self-incriminations, and not implored her with ever-increasing intensity to join him in them. Mailman's wife was fairly tolerant of others' foibles, provided they kept her out of it. But she did not want to picket convenience stores that stopped stocking Yoo-Hoo. She did not want to write daily letters of protest to foreign governments. She did not want to cover the windows with dark curtains and replace all the incandescent lightbulbs with fluorescent ones. She did not want to set fire to a stolen cache of Sears Christmas "Wish Books." And she had no desire whatsoever to encircle her house with low electrified fences to keep dogs from trespassing. In time, she would realize that she did not want to be married to Mailman, either, and that her own employer, the good-looking and perfectly well-adjusted Frank Payne, might serve as an excellent replacement.

Strictly speaking, Mailman's wife is no longer Mailman's wife.

Mailman has noticed lately that his wife and Dr. Payne have been receiving brochures and other correspondence relating to the adoption of poor children from distant lands, such as China and India. It appears that they have set in motion the process of bringing such a child to the United States to be raised. Many times, Mailman's wife had suggested to Mailman that the best way to protest the foreign governments whose policies and customs he so virulently abhorred might be to take in a needy child suffering from the effects of those very policies and customs, and it seems this is exactly what Mailman's wife is planning to do with Dr. Payne. Mailman's feelings about this are complex, and so that he doesn't spiral into confusion and misery trying to sort them out, he has put them out of his mind.

J . R O B E R T   L E N N O N

Mailman's Truck

After he leaves the coffee shop, Mailman determines that to go home would simply be too depressing, and he drives his truck to the drive-up window of a popular fast-food restaurant and orders a hamburger and french fries. The hamburger and fries go down with difficulty, not only because of Mailman's sensitive stomach but because of his cognizance of the deforestation of the Brazilian rain forest due to the cattle ranching that provides the all-beef patty. He is parked in the restaurant parking lot, just off the county highway, and since it is rush hour a steady stream of traffic flows noisily past. Mailman leaves the truck running so that he can listen to talk radio. There is a call-in show about strange phenomena on now, about which, Mailman, a scientist at heart, has mixed feelings. On the one hand, Mailman requires proof of a thing to believe it; on the other hand, he wishes the incredible things he hears were true. Alien spaceships. Cattle mutilations. Civilizations on Mars. Structures on the moon. Abominable snowmen. Sasquatches. Mailman screams at the callers, berating them for their gullibility, and turns up the volume so that he can hear above the sounds of traffic and of his own screaming voice.

After the show is over and darkness has begun to fall, he drives to the outskirts of town, buys gasoline (he can fill up for free at the P.O., but since he's using the truck for nonpostal purposes, which is not actually permitted, he figures the least he can do is pay for fuel), and is the first to arrive at the drive-in theater, where tonight there will be a double feature, a brand-new action-adventure picture starring Harrison Ford and a revival of *Taxi Driver*. The child who mans the ticket booth recognizes him and greets him with a manly nod. Mailman pays, pulls up to his favorite spot (dead center of the lot, about a hundred feet from the screen), and climbs into the back of the truck to wait.

He has altered the truck to better suit his needs. Metal shelves with a two-inch lip serve to keep plastic crates of mail from falling to the floor, and the remaining space is taken up by a folding lawn chair and a low table, where he keeps a lot of magazines he has stolen from his customers. *Scientific American*. *Soldier of Fortune*. *Popular Mechanics*. *People*. He picks up a recent *People* and reads an article about the very movie he's about to see. Ford plays an environmentalist whose life is threatened when he discovers that a mining company owned by wealthy Germans has been destroying wildlife along a length of Alaskan shoreline. There is apparently a frenzied chase on Jet Skis and a passionate love scene with a beautiful Native American activist.

There used to be a little cot in here, hung on metal hooks from the wall of the truck, which Mailman used for morning naps back when he couldn't sleep at night. He foolishly left it here when he quit and his replacement removed it (though for some reason the magazines and table and chair remained). For a while the cot also served as the site of an affair he conducted with a fellow postal employee, a young woman named Lori, who sorted mail in the morning for the carriers, then filled post-office boxes. One morning, after several days of glances exchanged between herself and Mailman, Lori came out to the loading dock carrying Mailman's mail, hoisted it into his truck, and then climbed in after it. This went on each morning for several weeks, until P.O. box customers began to complain of late delivery, at which time the P.O. hired a spy to work the P.O. box area, and the spy promptly caught Lori sneaking away, and she was fired. Mailman, for his part, was simply suspended without pay for one week, as nobody had complained about any lapse of service on his route, and Lori herself denied that Mailman had any involvement in her delinquency. Though this was manifestly false, it probably helped to save Mailman's job.

Mailman wished to thank her, but she vanished from town. Not long after, he began to steam open mail.

The Harrison Ford movie is no good. The Germans are unambiguously evil and Harrison Ford the reassuring embodiment of middle-class selflessness and responsibility. A maudlin score played in a minor key instructs the viewer in the proper emotions. Mailman is so bored that he falls asleep and completely misses *Taxi Driver*. He is awakened by the sounds of teenagers revving their engines and watches the credits roll to the very end. He is the last to leave.

Before going home he drives the truck around the Grape Street complex to see if Jenny Vandermeer's light is on. It is. Against his better judgment he parks on the street half a block away and watches her through the trees. She is walking around in her kitchen, making food. It is after midnight, and he wonders what she could be making at this hour, warm milk or cocoa, perhaps, to help her sleep, or maybe she was busy today and has only now found the time to eat dinner.

Some time later she comes to the window and stares out into the night, and he enjoys the sight of her face for some long seconds before he realizes that she is looking directly at him. This gives him a fright. He had felt, parked here in his mail truck (an item so ubiquitous that it is essentially invisible) that he was impervious to observation.

Not after midnight, though.

Mailman's Parents

God help them, they are alive. They live in Florida, a place Mailman happens to hate, if for no other reason than that his parents, given their age, are statistically likely to live there, and by living there have thoughtlessly embraced the status quo. This is perhaps the only way, however, his parents embrace the status quo. His father is a mechanical engineer and his mother a former dancer. They used to live in Newark, New Jersey, where the family cellar was cluttered with peculiar specialized tools and tiny pieces of metal in various shapes, the family walls covered with photographs of his mother posing in tights and evening gowns with various men besides his father, and the family cabinets stuffed with love letters from these men, along with other kinds of memorabilia. Somehow they have remained married for fifty-nine years, despite Mailman's mother's apparent infidelity and Mailman's father's unimpressive rate of success with his inventions. This is not to say that his father fails to create the devices he sets out to, but only that once he completes them he usually learns that they have already been invented by someone else. His father's avocation (which is how Mailman thinks of it) is funded by a pension from a large corporation that chose generously to offer him early retirement, instead of summary dismissal, when he grew eccentric. This same money financed the purchase of the tiny bungalow he shares with Mailman's mother, and pays for Mailman's mother's hairdresser's appointments, which add up to two or three a week, spread over a large number of hair-care establishments.

Today a letter arrived from Mailman's father, and now, settled in the gunmetal folding chair of the mail room at home, Mailman steams it open. He is in the habit of steaming open his own mail. This way the envelopes, resealed, remain tidy, saving space in the mail archive, and besides, they are good practice for steaming open other people's mail.

Dear Albert

Working on a new sort of cruise control for cars. Wrote Ford Corp but they claim no interest. Drafting letters to other "Big 3," also Japs. Mother got herself kicked out of Goodwill for stealing dress, except she just tried it on and forgot she was wearing it, so now I have to drive her all the way down to Sarasota Salv Arm because the bus leaves too early for there. While she shops I go to Ringling Museum and inspect Goya. They knew how to paint back then.

Yours Dad

Mailman gets several of these each week. It used to bother him that his father didn't just save up his thoughts over two or three weeks, then write a decent letter, but these days Mailman likes getting the little updates, and besides, he can't complain, as he only sends them cards at Christmas and their birthdays (and once a cheap old brittle postcard from Belarus with a picture of Lenin's interred body on it) and calls them perhaps once every two months.

Mailman remembers his father meeting him daily at the bus stop after school, and how it embarrassed him, Mailman, among his friends, as his father would immediately, often from half a block away, begin to report in great detail the results of the day's experimentation, talking with

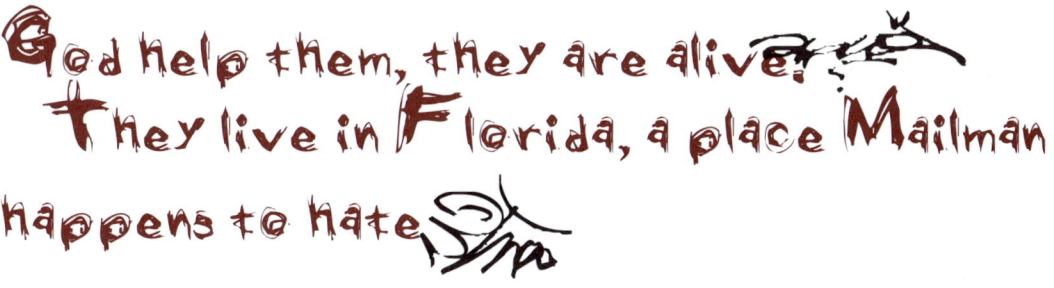

greater intensity and animation the further he walked, reeking of nervous sweat and metallic dust, and though the experiments interested Mailman greatly and he loved his father dearly, it impressed his young friends with the sense that Mailman's father, and by association Mailman, was insane. And though he did not lose his friends over this misunderstanding, it caused them to keep Mailman at arms' length, and none of them ever visited his home or engaged in the entertainments Mailman suggested, no matter how appealing they might otherwise be.

It was Mailman himself who would chase them away, eventually, as they came to be interested in girls. Though the thought of sex titillated him, the endless discussion of its many elements disgusted him, and the inflated claims of experience with it disappointed him. In fact, it would not be until he met his wife that Mailman would make love with a woman for the first time, and though sex made him embarrassed and sometimes even terrified, he missed doing it, the way one might miss a drunken uncle, now dead, who, though he sometimes lost his head and socked you, was still the funniest and most charming person you'd ever met.

Mailman's Dream

That night Mailman has a dream. In it, he and his wife and Dr. Payne are on vacation together, the three of them, at some kind of luxurious resort, the kind doctors stay at, with an eighteen-hole golf course, tennis courts, several large swimming pools, a gourmet restaurant and bar, and a good mile of private beach on which wealthy guests in various states of undress loll around spending money. Considering Mailman's wife has brought Dr. Payne along, Mailman is having a pretty good time. The three of them sun themselves by a pool and play a round of golf, each stroke of which Mailman, who does not play golf, sees and feels with perfect clarity. The ball leaps off his clubs as if by magic, whisking through the air with a kind of intelligence, homing in on the greens. The weather is beautiful.

After a rich dinner the three of them head off to the beach for an evening swim. At the water's edge, Mailman's wife and Dr. Payne take off their clothes and, naked, jump into the surf. Mailman is a little bit disgusted, even as he is aroused by the sight of his wife's body, which he hasn't seen in a while. He realizes that he has been wearing his postal uniform and a bulging sack of mail is slung over his shoulder.

When they get out of the water, Mailman's wife and Dr. Payne hold a whispered conference and approach Mailman with grave faces. They tell him they have had a good time with him, but that he is being rude to his date and he really should pay her a little more attention.

Date?

Yes, says his wife. You're really ignoring her. She and Dr. Payne are shooting little glances at his mail bag.

Mailman looks down and sees that his bag is not filled with mail, but in fact contains Lori, the postal employee with whom he once had a brief affair, curled up into a little fetal ball. He bends over, trying to get a closer look in there. He says her name, but there is no response.

It dawns on him that his inattention has come at terrible cost. He has kept her balled up all day long, and now he has killed her.

Mornings, Mailman eats: yogurt, granola, fruit, wheat germ, juice. But first he chews and swallows raw a small handful of brown rice, which is supposed to cleanse the system, according to a macrobiotic cookbook he once read, which elsewhere also said that tomatoes were evil, which a small part of him still believes to this day. The brown rice is stored in a little Tupperware vessel on his bedside table, next to the pile of folded handkerchiefs and clock radio, and after he consumes his morning handful he listens to half an hour of news, then gets up and eats the rest of his breakfast.

Mailman's shower broke some years ago, and since then he has only taken baths. He ought to be able to fix this problem in under a minute, but instead has gotten used to it and rather likes the ritual. He runs a bath while he relieves himself on the toilet, then bathes for twenty minutes while reading a stolen magazine, brushes his teeth, applies deodorant (not antiperspirant, which contains aluminum and is said to cause Alzheimer's disease), dresses in his postal uniform, and leaves the house.

This morning he shivers as he dons his uniform, recalling the dream of the night before.

It is a light mail day. Few new catalogs have come out, and few magazines. It doesn't take long to sort, steam open, and photocopy the desired letters, and he has nearly finished delivering by two-thirty. Around this time he arrives at the Grape Street complex and, remembering his strange encounter the night before with Jenny Vandermeer, calmly stuffs the mail into the building's rack of boxes. He collects outgoing letters from the ledge above the boxes and returns to his truck, checking to see if anything interesting is afoot. Something is. It's a postcard from Jenny, addressed to Professor Mark. It tells him she is coming to see him in a few days. And then, at the bottom, it says this, in a postscript:

I hope this gets to you. Something weird is going on with my mail.

Mailman's Plan

It isn't until late that night, while he's poring over the goings-on of the neighborhood (Rachel, the new mother, has finally gotten into a fight with her sister, MaryJane, the one she thinks is kind of a slut), that he gets the idea. He roots through the file cabinet and comes up with the Jenny Vandermeer file and studies the letters from Professor Mark. The professor is none too consistent. He sometimes writes by hand and sometimes types. Sometimes, but not often, he works on a computer (the computer is in his office) and prints out the letters on a printer. It is this last method that will allow Mailman to carry out his plan. He rereads all of Professor Marks letters to Jenny, noting the frequent use of certain phrases ("as a matter of fact," "consequently," "without a doubt," "that really burns my ass") and common variations in sentence length. He takes out a legal pad and drafts a letter to Jenny, from Professor Mark, confessing his love for another woman closer to his own age and imploring her to stop writing, for her own good. "As a matter of fact," reads the letter, "Nancy and I are moving in together. Consequently your letters will not even reach me. Without a doubt, its best that we cut off communication entirely. Sincerely."

Next morning Mailman moves his routine up by an hour and reports to the P.O. early. There is a computer and printer in the back office, where telephone calls are fielded and complaints processed, and Mailman starts it up and pokes around on the word processor, which he has used a couple of times, for a typeface similar to the one Professor Mark uses on his computer-composed letters. Sure enough, the very same typeface is available. He types the letter into the computer carefully, checks the spelling with the built-in checker, and prints out a copy. He practices, practices, hastily signs. It looks very much like something Professor Mark, he of the burnt ass, might print out himself, in his little office at Yale, under the conspiratorial eye of the lithe yet mature Nancy, who is already reaching for the good professor's zipper even as he's affixing a stamp onto the envelope.

Which envelope Mailman takes his sweet time preparing, prudently copying Jenny's and Professor Mark's addresses onto the blank face. He botches several envelopes (they are security envelopes, with blue static on the inside, just like Prof M uses) before getting one right, the t's that aren't quite crossed, the wind-eroded r's, the i's with a gap in the middle, like the grin of a six-year-old. He digs out one of the obscure Fulbright Scholarship stamps the professor has been using since they were issued a good two years before and self-adheres it to the upper right, slightly crooked, slapdash really, the way you'd expect a person whose brain is all too preoccupied with the highfalutin' concerns of his area of study to apply postage. He adds a one-cent stamp to account for the rate hike. And then the cancel. He sneaks out to the counter and grabs a rubber stamp, adjusts the date to a couple of days before, then sticks a bit of discarded self-adhesive paper over the name of the city. He inks the stamp, pulls off the sticky, and thunks down on the crooked Fulbright. Where the name of the city ought to have been is an illegible smear, only enough to establish that yes, this letter did originate in a city of some kind, hard to tell really which city, but one might naturally assume New Haven, Connecticut. The university post office, perhaps, at a certain institute of higher learning.

By now it's time to load up the truck, and Mailman is experiencing an unfamiliar kind of light-headedness, a sort of etherized dizzy calm, a just-gave-blood feeling, which would be disturbing if it weren't so *wonderful,* and he realizes that this feeling is, in fact, *elation.* He is so excited that he forgoes his usual break and delivers the mail without opening it first, and he rushes through his route at breakneck speed, fudging stop signs and traffic lights, nearly upsetting his mail cart on familiar sidewalk hazards and flaws, so that he inadvertently arrives at the Grape Street complex at exactly the time Jenny Vandermeer is returning home for lunch.

Early today, she says.

I'm playing in a soccer tournament, blurts Mailman, and if I'm not there by one-thirty my team is going to lose the championship.

It's very important, Mailman continues.

I play defensive wing, Mailman concludes.

She betrays no prior knowledge of soccer that would reveal his own total ignorance of the sport, and she is staring openly at the pile of mail in his hand, which reminds him of the terrible dream, and the way his wife and Dr. Payne glanced at the deadly mailbag. He clears his throat.

Anything for number eight? she is asking.

He removes *the letter* and hands it to her, and her eyebrows arch as she reads the return address. Then he remembers she has other mail and hands that to her, too, which she accepts with a quizzical smile, and she thanks him and turns to go inside and he forces himself to open the rack of boxes and fill them with everybody else's mail.

About Mail

Why mail?

It seemed to Mailman, on his first day of delivering mail (August 14, 1968), that the responsibility was too great for any one man to shoulder, and that this job, which had seemed so simple, so idyllic in description, was in fact the worst possible enterprise for a mathematician recovering from a nervous breakdown. Theorizing about the origin of the universe may well have proved his undoing, but the universe was indifferent to his hypothesis and had continued to exist despite his failure.

Mail, on the other hand, *must go through*.

Who questions mail? No one. Regardless of the weather, mail comes. In prosperity and poverty, mail comes, mail comes. At a set time every weekday and Saturday (excepting national holidays), every citizen opens his mailbox and removes from it the day's mail. Perhaps a citizen would be shocked to find that his mail hasn't come: we'll never know, because *it always does*.

This consistency is the work not of machines, but men.

August 14 was a hot, hot day. You may consult your almanac. Mailman's armpits became drenched with sweat, the headband of Mailman's hat, the small of Mailman's back; for the love of God, Mailman's crotch. His hands left soaking creases in the mail. The ink from magazines and catalogs coated his fingers and made its way onto his customers' personal letters. And unlike the universe, his customers noticed. They asked him if he was all right. Several offered him iced tea or lemonade (which he accepted: a mistake: his bladder filled to bursting, and there was nowhere to empty it). He realized that their correspondence—their primary contact with the people they loved—was literally in his hands. Primitive man had communicated by speech alone, with no one needed to ferry the words from one person to the next. But Mailman, fully modern, a vital gear in this vast contraption, *was* needed to do exactly that.

To be back in the world of perfect abstractions! He would return, Mailman then believed, he would return.

Today Mailman sees that the universe is adaptable; it heals its wounds. The space-time continuum is rent; the space-time continuum is mended. The same is true in the world of men. When he has to destroy letters, what are the consequences?

There are no consequences.

People get over it. There may be some misunderstanding, perhaps even some weeks of pain, of misplaced resentment or confusion or misery. But then the writer tries again. Didn't you get my last letter? the writer asks. Why no, comes the reply, it must have got lost in the mail. And all is well again. And if by chance all is not well—if an affair is broken, if a fortune is lost, if the recipient, believing himself forgotten, is moved to take his own life—well:

People get over it.

This is not, however, what Mailman is thinking that night, when the telephone rings and Jenny Vandermeer's voice identifies itself on the other end.

Is this Albert Lippincott? she sweetly inquires.

He's not in.

You're my mailman, Mr. Lippincott.

I think you have the wrong number.

There is a deathly pause. A black breeze pushes its way into his kitchen, where he is halfway through a large bowl of Cheerios in skim milk, and the hairs on his arm stand at horrified attention.

Mr. Lippincott, whispers Jenny Vandermeer, *the jig is up*.

Mailman's Mistake

Of course, when your sometime lover and regular correspondent who you were about to hop a plane to go visit suddenly dumps you with a brusque and awkward letter laying forth an extremely implausible explanation, you immediately *call him on the phone*.

Mailman's Flight

Mailman's wife is not especially surprised to see him, even now, late at night, when Dr. Payne typically begins his Nurse, bring me a whiskey, Nurse, touch me here please routine. The two of them were just settling down for their evening of gross anatomy when a knock came on the door, not a ring, and she knew it was Mailman because the doorbell hasn't worked on *his* house for eight years, and in Mailman's little world, if one doorbell doesn't work, no doorbells at any houses anywhere in America work. Mailman's face is stricken and gray and he is carrying a little suitcase and a brown paper grocery sack roughly rolled at the top.

Albert!

I'm just wondering if I could stay here for the night, it's no big deal, there's just a little problem at the house, it's nothing really, and I just need a place to stay for just a short time.

Frank is on his feet, all shaggy nods and handshakes, and to Mailman's credit he takes Frank's hand and grips it with something resembling firmness, and Frank fixes him a whiskey which Mailman, seated now, accepts but does not drink. The dogs come loping up to him and he bristles but stands his ground, and Frank orders them away after they've gotten a few good sniffs of Mailman's privates. She notices there's something different about him and it takes her a few minutes to realize that he isn't wearing his postal uniform. She has not seen him in his civvies for some time.

The three of them quietly watch television. Every couple of minutes Frank tries to draw Mailman out, but Mailman, sitting over there in the La-Z-Boy, is having none of it; he smiles politely, then peers into the paper bag and back to the television, where there is a news story on about bicycle theft. Not much later Frank announces he has a lot of patients in the morning, which he is making up, and bids them both good night and shakes Mailman's hand one last time and retires to the bedroom. Over the sounds of the TV she can hear him putting on his pajamas and climbing into bed, and then the snick of the lamp being turned off. She turns to her former husband.

Albert?

There is no response save for a barely perceptible shaking of the head. It is obvious that he has done something irresponsible and that his life has forever changed. She tells him he can stay as long as he has to, and if he needs anything, money, food, whatever, she is there for him.

His answer surprises her: Go to bed. He needs you more than I do. And then, as she reaches for the remote control, adds: I'll leave before you get up.

The TV goes dark and she sets down the remote.

All right, she says, and goes.

In bed, with Frank's arms around her, she sees that she has gotten her wish, and Mailman is forever gone from her life. She won't hear from him ever again. There are only the small sounds of his presence in the next room, and that's all there will ever be. It is enough to make her momentarily sad, but she is tired, and before long she has fallen asleep.

For this reason she doesn't see Mailman's face in the doorway, illuminated every few seconds by the headlights of passing cars, as he watches her sleeping in the embrace of Dr. Frank Payne. She never used to sleep this way with Mailman, or rather, Mailman never embraced her this way, always conscious of the sanctity of sleep, of how irritated it would make him to be groped, grabbed, fondled, or otherwise impeded in his effort to rest. Nevertheless, her face is calm and, in the nearly nonexistent light, smooth and unlined as a child's.

This thought—the thought of his wife as a child—reminds him of a fantasy he once entertained when they were married and which he never confessed to her, as the admission would only have embarrassed her, and anyway she would have been powerless to fulfill it. The fantasy was that he, Mailman, could travel back in time to January of 1951, to the maternity ward of a hospital in Ames, Iowa, and hold in his arms for just a few seconds the newborn version of his wife. He'd seen pictures: the round shouting head, the disproportionate neck and shoulders and belly he would one day press his mouth to; it was not hard to imagine the scant weight of her, the hummingbird heart, her cries. He'd just walk in and pick her up. Nobody would stop him. The fantasy, back in the days when he used to entertain it, was so palpable, so intensely imagined that now, standing in her bedroom doorway, he finds it hard to believe that it never actually happened.

When she stirs and rolls to face her husband, Mailman shuts the door and returns to the kitchen, where he has been counting and recounting his money, which is in cash and is everything he has now. Words like *mail fraud* and *mandatory sentencing* pass through his mind. When he's through counting he empties the paper bag onto the table and reads again every letter his father has ever sent him, and smells their pages for traces of sweat and burnt metal, which with his eyes closed he can make out, barely. He'll give himself forty-five minutes to make the furtive walk to the bus station, and by tomorrow afternoon he'll be in Denver, and by the week's end, Florida, where important work is being done that requires his assistance.

Vanity, vanity

MARGE PIERCY

Who can explain what a mother's
vanity means to a girl child?
It was magic, destiny,
it was her in a shiny slippery slip
unlike my plain cotton undies
putting on her face.

But she had a face every day
beautiful as the marigold of the sun
warming my flesh, bright
enough to blind me to others.
She rose every day over me.
She put me into darkness at night.

Still this was magic, scented sprays,
opaque liquids, pale powders
floating in the air around her
as she patted and pawed at herself.
Gold colored lipstick tubes
smudged grease on my fingers.

A big bottle of Mille Fleurs stood
in the dead center of chaos
back against the mirror.

Vanity, vanity

Older than me, where had it
come from? One of her brothers
I think. Never from father

who if he gave her anything
would produce a broom, an iron.
Her little implements suggested
esoteric rituals of cuticles
and nails she never performed,
hands smooth as riverworn rocks

with washing, scrubbing, nails
broken, always a network of
scratches, scars. Yet when
she sat at her vanity in her
pearly slip shining like moonlight
and painted on her smiling face

for company, for dinner out,
for some rare treat, how she
shone. Rising, how she glittered,
light breaking on the beads
of her dress as if it scattered
on shattered ice of a river

released by a sudden thaw.
*I am not despised, I am not
the wife of a house,* her
posture sang: For a moment
the mirror gave her the past
before she married into dust.

Chickadee

Ed Ochester

Late at night when the house is silent

I'll put down my book and quarter an apple

or put a few slivers of cheese on a piece

of flatbread, and it must be the poverty

of those meals which makes me think

of the departed, like the old German

who used to walk hunched every afternoon

past my window when I was very small

and wave to me, his walrus moustache

yellowed by cigars (back then all the old

men smoked and they lived forever)

which he held in an amber mouthpiece.

No one in my house knew him, but he waved

just the same, and tapped his cane toward

the corner where the cop stood directing

traffic, but stopped long enough to

tip his cap to the old man, as though

it were a Bing Crosby movie and not

CHICKADEE

a lousy corner in Queens on an eight-lane
boulevard. And I think again of Fat Charley,
his huge head—thin black hair parted down
the middle—floating above his beer stein,
and his terrible jokes—every 4th of July:
"the blessings of liberty for ourselves
and our posteriors"—and again of my father
walking dark tenement streets in Brooklyn,
collecting crumpled bills from the poor
for their small policies, life & casualty.

I'm sick of pity because it's
always self-referential. This morning,
this warm day in March 500 miles from that
corner in the city, I listened to the birds
in the hawthorn—such singing, and snow is
expected—such difficult lives. One chickadee
came close to inspect me, hopping from
branch to branch to get a better view, until
I could see her carpet-tack beak as she
studied me, cool and fearless, this creature
that weighs an ounce, with her merciless
black-bead reptilian eye.

New Voice

Road

JAMES CONRAD

A HIGH-SCHOOL ENGLISH TEACHER ONLY HAS SO MANY CHANCES IN LIFE TO GET OUT, AND I TOOK MINE THE MOMENT IT CAME. EVEN THOUGH I HAD MET MY GODMOTHER ONLY TWICE, I HAD KEPT UP WITH CARDS FOR CHRISTMAS AND HER BIRTHDAY, AND THIS, APPARENTLY, WAS ENOUGH FOR HER TO WILL ME A HUNDRED THOUSAND DOLLARS' WORTH OF STOCKS AND BONDS.

I sat on the portfolio for a few months, expecting her relatives to materialize in the parking lot of Hopkins High School at the end of the day and serve me papers challenging the inheritance. My old high-school girlfriend, Brenda, checked things out for a minimal fee.

"There seems to have been enough money to go around," she told me over a celebratory lunch. "Quit worrying, it's yours. Just don't fuck it up."

"How do you mean?" I hadn't seen Brenda since our senior year. I remembered my mother nagging me that she had moved back from Chicago and was a successful lawyer now and that I was too late, she had already married. Brenda had aged in that way girls from Minnesota tend to age. Hair still blonde, though you couldn't tell whether it was helped with chemicals, slightly plumper around the neck from the extremely rich diet of the state, but her body still fit, most likely a jogger with a gym membership. Her skin looked as smooth as it had been when I had last kissed it that summer after graduation.

"Don't head off to Europe or Mexico. It's a lot of money, but it's not that much money. Do you own anything, Mark? Do you even own that ridiculous blue thing you drove up in? You're thirty-five, right? You probably don't own a thing on the planet." She was twisting the straw around in the ice of her empty sea breeze and I stared helplessly at her enormous wedding ring. Despite my continual suggestions of ordering another round, she had declined and now seemed to be trying to scoop out any last drops of the vodka. "Why don't you start with a decent car? Then I'd suggest a down payment on a house. Or, better yet, do absolutely nothing with any of it. They're good stocks. Shove it in a drawer and forget about it until you retire."

I was staring at her out of an old habit, trying to figure out how to seduce her at one-thirty in the afternoon on a Tuesday in March. She had taken off her suit jacket and the buttons of her silk shirt seemed like they could fall open upon contact. When do you ever stop presuming a physical intimacy with an old lover, I thought as she looked across the table at me in confusion about my silence. Later on I wondered if I should have felt ashamed of exposing my nonexistent financial situation to an ex-girlfriend who now seemed to have it all. I'd missed an opportunity—bored career woman gets real with high-school boyfriend turned high-school English teacher. I didn't get the chance to find out.

"I gotta get back," she said, standing up and pulling her suit coat on. "Hey, what are you doing still single? Do you have someone stashed away you're not telling me about? You're keeping something from me, I still know you well enough."

February 10, 1998
Dear Mark,
I had this dream last night that the two of us were on this ship wearing formal clothes and it was night and there were a million stars out and even though it was winter and really cold, we didn't seem to mind as we walked along the deck alone. Suddenly, we hit this iceberg and the ship was suddenly the Titanic *and everyone was panicking and running around us and the captain walked by and you grabbed his arm and said, "Why are we just sitting here? Why don't you floor it and take us in the direction of the nearest ship coming our way and we'll meet halfway?" The captain said something about how that would rip the ship in two and kill everyone and then*

> I WAS STARING AT HER OUT OF AN OLD HABIT, TRYING TO FIGURE OUT HOW TO SEDUCE HER AT ONE-THIRTY IN THE AFTERNOON ON A TUESDAY IN MARCH.

you said, "Well why don't we all start getting on this iceberg that we crashed into and wait there until help arrives," and the captain said something about how that wouldn't hold us up. Then he told me I had to get into a lifeboat with all the women and children, but I refused, so when the captain wasn't looking, you lifted me up and over the railing onto the iceberg and then you got on it with me and we made ourselves comfortable and watched as the ship slowly sank. Isn't that funny? It made me think of when we went to see Titanic *and how I cried and loved it so much and how surprised I was after when you told me you hated it. Anyway, I know you also hate hearing people's dreams, but I just woke up from it and wrote this all out so I wouldn't forget and I'm sending it anyway.*

Love, Kelly

P.S. Don't forget, I'll be in town next month.

"Which Hanson are you?" Lou asked at the Andree Post Office five miles down the road from my new house. Lou seemed to be the sole government employee of the post office. It was no bigger than the smaller of my two bedrooms, which I was planning to use as an office. He

Lou looked at me seriously, like he was the mayor and town council rolled into one and couldn't digest the idea that such a significant land transaction had taken place behind his back.

was a small guy with a large mustache that seemed to overwhelm his face, and though he looked ten years older than me, I guessed we were the same age.

"Not a Hanson at all. Bill Hanson sold me the place," I said, and pushed forward my completed application for a post-office box. Lou looked down at my name as if he didn't believe me. "The Hansons big around here?"

"They own about the whole western side of Gooseberry Lake. I had no idea they were cutting it up." Lou looked at me seriously, like he was the mayor and town council rolled into one and couldn't digest the idea that such a significant land transaction had taken place behind his back. He quickly smiled once my own expression became as serious as his. "What brings you up to this area then, family?"

"Finally decided to get away from the city. Got a writing project and thought some peace and quiet would help."

"You couldn't have picked a better time than April to move in," Lou said with a slight smile.

"The Hansons come up here still?"

"You haven't met Ethel?" he said, his smile gone.

"No, but I'm sure I will when I'm up here full time by the end of May."

"Oh yes, you will." Lou put my application in a shoebox and gave me a key. "The Carrutherses have the meadow and woods on the other side of you. They're quite nice, though neither of them get around much anymore. But if you have any trouble, just call on them, they'd be glad to help you out."

I thanked Lou and left. Outside the sun was slowly working down the piles of snow that had turned black from salt and sand. Thousands of razor-thin streams cut across the roads and sidewalks and birds hopped among the naked branches above. The ice on the lake had shrunk back from the shore and had turned a purple bruise color. I knew by that weekend or the next it would be gone entirely.

Within days after Brenda advised me not to go to Europe or Mexico, I had called some Realtors about buying a house. I told them I wanted to be out of Minneapolis, near a lake if possible, and private, but when I told them my price limit was less than a hundred thousand they laughed and told me I could expect a long commute. Bill Hanson's place in Andree was the third one I looked at and, a two-hour drive from the city, the farthest out. But it had the lake and privacy, and with the school year coming to an end, I acted fast. Too fast, I now know, but at the time the excitement of actually owning every window, floorboard, shelf, tree, stone, and shingle of those six acres was enough for me to sell off half the stocks and bonds, give my notice to the school board, and wrap things up in four short weeks.

"You know you're remote when the place doesn't even have a for-sale sign," Brenda said the day we drove up to meet the surveyor. The property was off the county road, a half mile down a dirt road that then forked to the right, then went uphill another half mile through dense wood before opening onto a clearing where the house sat surrounded by a small lawn with a sweeping view of the lake. It was one of those rare summer days stuck in the middle of March and the sunlight felt like a hot shower. We decided the surveyor looked competent enough and was slightly annoyed by the two of us following him around, so we circled the lake while he did his job.

"I'm probably the only nibble they had. I'm sure you'd advise against such a purchase." Brenda had taken off her heavy wool sweater and tied it around her waist. We had left our coats in the car and both of us were squinting from the sun hitting us from all sides off the snow and ice.

"It's absolutely beautiful," she said, waving her arms at the lake and sky, woods and fields. "I just wonder what you're gonna do up here by yourself."

"There's that screenplay I always meant to finish." I said this carefully, fearful that she, like most everyone, would burst out laughing whenever a high-school English teacher used the words *my novel* or *my screenplay*. "You remember Philip, from the soccer team? He's some kind of accountant now for Paramount in L.A. He said he'd help me get it into the hands of some agents if I could get it done."

"What's it about?" Her question stopped me. It had been five years since I had looked at the ten pages of that screenplay, and no one I remembered had ever gone so far as to inquire more about it than the Philip part.

"Oh, love, sex, murder, aliens. Something for everyone."

"I think you should get a dog. It would be good company."

By the time we came full circle back to the house, it was almost dark and the surveyor was gone. What was left of the sun was blocked by pine trees and the temperature seemed to have dropped from July to January. But before I could put an arm around Brenda to rub her shoulders she ran ahead to her BMW to retrieve her coat.

Bill Hanson lived in Philadelphia and I had never met him. His lawyer took care of everything in Minneapolis with Brenda and, despite having to put nearly half the money down due to the fact that I owned nothing and was leaving my job, I came out of it confident I could properly budget myself and spend at least a year not worrying about money. I moved quickly, not wanting to deal with my friends or colleagues, not wanting to talk about the money or my vague plans. Of course Kelly had something to do with it too.

April 1, 1998
Dear Mark:
You're a complete idiot. I happen to like the University of Minnesota, besides, if it was good enough for you it's certainly good enough for me. My apartment overlooks the freeway but I've gotten used to the noise—I pretend it's the ocean when I'm studying or trying to fall asleep—and if you'd ever come and visit I could show you the bathtub with feet and the kitchen, which is bigger than my bedroom. Audrey is great as far as roommates go. She's never here and always asks in

advance when she wants to have friends over for dinner or drinks so I can figure out if I want to be here or not. I'm reading Faulkner like you always told me to. It seems to fit well with my mood this winter, lots of anger and passion, intensity in every person, place, and thing. I still have the copy of Absalom, Absalom! *you lent me once and then told me I could keep. I read from it randomly—it's always right by my bed. The camping trip we took to Lake Millacs last summer was one of the most perfect two days of my life, even if it did seem you spent more time trying to light a fire than pay attention to me (ha!). It felt so amazing to lie next to you in the complete open space, the sky and stars, and I didn't mean to start crying and freak you out, I was just so happy, and also sad that I wasn't going to be seeing you every day anymore. I think about that time a lot, do you? If you don't call me soon I swear I'll just show up in the school parking lot and sit on the hood of your car waiting for you to come out.*

Love,
Kel

"Get out of here! Get out of here!" I was in the kitchen making coffee when I heard the front door slam and a woman's voice shouting in the living room. I raced into the room in time to see the stray white cat that had moved in at the beginning of May, the month before, run out the front door the old woman was holding open. I felt like I needed no introduction.

"Is that your cat?" I asked, drying my hands on my jeans and trying to remember what state my hair and beard growth were in from the last time I had looked in a mirror. I had spent the last month in front of the cable TV, with occasional hikes, but the screenplay, when I did bother to look at it, seemed to be in a foreign language.

"Seems like it's yours now, and good riddance." She appeared barely five feet tall, although her posture was commanding for her age, which I judged to be anywhere from seventy to ninety. She wore loose-fitting khakis that were stuffed inside her hiking boots, a bright turquoise long-sleeved sweatshirt, and a bright orange shawl wrapped around her shoulders. Her hair was big, teased out, a wild mix of brown coloring

> I DIDN'T MEAN TO START CRYING AND FREAK YOU OUT, I WAS JUST SO HAPPY

> SHE IGNORED MY HAND AND WALKED PAST ME INTO THE ROOM, SURVEYING THE FURNITURE, NEWSPAPERS AND MAGAZINES

and natural gray, and she squinted at me through huge purple-tinted glasses.

"Mark Reilly," I said, approaching her with my hand out. "You must be Ethel Hanson."

She ignored my hand and walked past me into the room, surveying the furniture, newspapers and magazines, bookshelves and unpacked boxes. There was some furniture left when I moved in, which I had the option to keep or Bill Hanson's lawyer said he would remove. Most of it was antique and seemed to belong with the exposed wood walls and beamed ceilings, so I kept it.

"That's my lamp," she said, pointing at an old green-domed desk lamp I had moved out of the bedroom to a prominent place on the mantelpiece.

"You can take it," I said quickly, and she looked at me with a strange smile, as if she had been making a joke but was reconsidering.

"So how do you know my brother?" she asked.

"You mean Bill? I don't. Never met him." She let out a loud "ha" which made her cough. "Can I get you something to drink? Coffee, water, lemonade . . ."

"I'm not staying. I just had to come over and see for myself." She swept her arm grandly around the room and looked at me as if I was in on whatever it was she meant. "This house, this *property* has been in my family for years. Now I have a call in to Bill, but I really don't expect to hear back from him, as he hasn't spoken to me in ten years. That's why I thought maybe *you* would be able to explain to me just what he thinks he's doing pulling this out from under me like this. But I'll find out if I have to drive all the way out to Philadelphia and ask him in person. I'm sure you never planned to be caught in the middle of something like this, but caught you are." She glanced around the room again and dramatically shuddered. "I promised my daughters I wouldn't talk your ear off about any of this without them around, so I'm leaving. Why don't you come up to the house, say, the day after tomorrow, maybe they can explain things to you, since they don't think I'm capable of it."

She walked out the front door and I followed her onto the small covered porch. I had no idea what to say to anything she had said or how I was even supposed to say goodbye. I saw the stray cat on the roof of my Civic cleaning himself in the sun.

"What's the cat's name, ma'am?" I asked as she carefully stepped down the three steps from the porch.

She looked back at me as if I were crazy. Then she looked back at the Civic. "Get out of here! Get out of here!" she yelled, and, upon hearing it, Get-Out-of-Here jumped down from the car, ran through her legs and back into the house.

"So you're here," Ethel Hanson said from behind the screen door. When I had rounded the corner of the driveway and the house was still a few hundred yards away, she was already standing there as if I had tripped some hidden sensor walking to her house. "June! Come out, he's here!"

Ethel was joined by a younger woman who was drying her hands with a towel. She was the same height as Ethel and the only resemblance I could make out through the screen was her prominent nose and brow. She was fully gray, unlike her mother, and looked all of the ten years she must have been older than me.

"I'm Kate. Really, mother, step back and let the poor man in."

"Then who's June?" I asked as I passed between the screen door and Ethel, who hadn't really made much room for me and smiled at me as if I were wild game stepping into her trap.

"That's just what mother calls me," Kate explained, gesturing to the living room and escorting me in. "My husband and I stay out here for the month of June to help out, which makes my sister Beth July and my sister Meg August."

"That's nice," I said, sitting down on one of the overstuffed leather chairs. Kate sat on the opposite side of the huge stone fireplace and politely smiled.

"Mother, would you please get over here and sit down," she said, without taking her eyes from me. Ethel obediently shuffled over to the couch facing us and sat down.

"Would you like something to drink, Mister . . ."

"Mark, please. It was very nice of your mother to invite me over. I've been anxious to meet my neighbors."

Ethel let out a low grunt and Kate kept her eyes pinned on me. I had the distinct feeling I shouldn't mutter any more pleasantries, as the meeting was only that, a meeting.

"I don't know what my mother has told you, but this land, you see, nearly this whole end of the lake, has been in our family since my grandfather came over from Hungary." Kate twisted the dishrag around in her hands and stared at it as she spoke. Ethel was still smiling at me and nodding her head at every word. "My uncle Bill, well we haven't really spoken to him in years, and his selling the house, your house, has been quite a shock to us."

"June's house," Ethel spat out. Kate paused, obviously trying to find words, and looked over at her, her eyes observing her mother in a sleepy way as she pressed her index finger up against her own lips. She reminded me of a woman I had dated a few years back. Although older than me, she looked my age. Yet I always imagined her becoming like Kate Hanson was now, her hair dry and gray, loosely held back by a rubber band, and her skin loose and trembling as she allowed herself to lose her own will, preoccupied with taking care of an aging parent.

"Why didn't you buy it?" I said.

"Buy it? It's ours!" Ethel flew off the couch and Kate quickly stood up and stepped over to her, her hands on her mother's shoulders, whispering something in her ear. Ethel sat down like a delinquent child and turned her body away from both of us.

"You see," Kate resumed, taking the seat next to me. "This is all rather emotional for us. I guess it never occurred to any of us that Uncle Bill would just sell the property like that. My grandfather split this place between the two of them, my mother and her brother. But Bill has lived out east for as long as I can remember and hasn't been up here since . . ." She glanced over at Ethel for help, but Ethel was still pretending she wasn't listening to us. "We've just presumed he'd hand the little lake house over one of these days, and my husband and I had planned on retiring there in a few years so we could be close to Mother. You can see then, this is all rather delicate."

The room felt extremely heavy. Dark wood walls, beamed ceiling, stone fireplace, dark leather furniture, and a deep burgundy rug. The windows were small squares that seemed to avoid the sunlight and were closed, which kept the room cooler than the humid day outside, but somehow had the effect of making everything hotter because of the lack of circulation. Ethel had turned around on the couch to be more comfortable but still wouldn't look at me, and I had the feeling she would refuse to look at me for the rest of the time I was there. Kate preferred looking down at her hands while I turned all the information she had just given me around in my mind like the stones I had picked up along the shore of the lake, bright vivid colors when I'd first seen them wet that turned into a dull brown as they dried. I stood up and Kate stood up with me.

"I welcome you to look at any paperwork you need to, but I can tell you there's nothing there that will help you," I said in my best schoolteacher tone.

"I appreciate that," she said, meeting my eyes. "And you're right, it won't help."

As I started walking to the door Ethel suddenly jumped up.

"The road," she said to her daughter, and I waited at the screen door, looking back at Kate. "Yes," Kate said, stepping up to me. "There's the matter of the road."

April 15, 1998
Dear Mark,
I'm sitting at Dudley's Coffeehouse between classes watching all these forgotten hippies trying to figure out tax forms—not like they have any money to pay the government with anyway. Thank God my mother takes care of all that for me. I just have to sign a couple things and it's done. She's still a little mad about me transferring schools and everything, but I kind of think she at least likes having me nearby. She's all over me about what I'm taking. She seems to think that if I don't come out of this with a business or law degree I'll turn into one of these hippies hiding from the IRS.

IT WAS PROBABLY ANY BORING DAY, BUT AT LEAST I SAW YOU AND PERHAPS YOU STARED AT ME IN THAT WAY THAT TOLD ME EVERYTHING I NEEDED TO KNOW

I understand that we can't see each other and even though you say we should just both move on from that separately, I don't really want to. I do think of you a little less frequently but if you suddenly walked in right now, I know that I'd be back thinking about you every five minutes again. I even went on a date last weekend—well, not really a date. It was a friend of Audrey's and we went as a foursome with her boyfriend to see a concert at Crazyquilt. It was fun, but I don't know. You probably think I'm trying to make you jealous or something—if I thought I could I wouldn't be writing this letter at all.

I can't help always thinking about things in terms of a year ago, what we were doing a year ago from today. It was probably any boring day, but at least I saw you and perhaps you stared at me in that way that told me everything I needed to know. Everyone's after me to cut my hair and I *think I don't do it because I remember how much you liked it long, how you'd tell me that. Write me, like you promised. I'm fine, but I still miss you.*

Yours,

K

Jogging became my solution to the TV addiction. By running nearly five miles a day, my body would retain slight pains around my muscles and joints that would make sitting on my couch uncomfortable. I kept moving until evening and started clearing out some of the scraggly land around the house. I had plans to till it and plant grass. I also started to spend time at the gardening store in town trying to figure out what would grow in the garden along the side of the house, which had obviously been let go years ago.

My favorite part of the jog was the last mile, the half-mile of dirt road I shared with the Hansons and the final half-mile of my own driveway, ending at the lake, where I'd kick off my tennis shoes and socks and peel off my sweat-soaked T-shirt before jumping into the cool water. The road was a confused zigzag through dense wood, made even harder to navigate by the number of potholes, which made me think it hadn't been graveled since Grandpa Hanson first showed up at Gooseberry Lake and started pulling out the trees by hand. At some angles, large pine branches would slap my car, and I always feared I'd drive up while a Hanson was driving down, forcing one of us to back out because the road could only fit one vehicle in its pronounced ruts. Of course, after what Kate Hanson had told me, I now feared running into a Hanson even more.

The half-mile from the county road to the fork where our two driveways separated was all on Ethel's land. Kate, somewhat reluctantly, passed along Ethel's decree that I was not to use it.

I must have laughed, because Ethel spun around and repeated exactly what Kate had just said, but with full fury. At that I walked out, deciding it wasn't anything to really worry about, that Ethel and Bill would eventually have it out over the phone and the attention would be taken off me.

A few days later, after I had already driven to town and back a few times, I slept in late and spent most of the day reading until I finally got the craving to turn on the television around six. I put my tennis shoes on instead. After jogging far out and taking time to soak my feet in the lake a few miles from home, I realized it was getting near eight and I should get back before dark. When I turned off the county road I was amazed at how dark the shared driveway was in the dense wood. I had trouble avoiding potholes and finally, just a few yards from the fork, my right foot fell directly into one. In an instant I was flat on my face with a burning sensation in my knees, elbows, and chin. I rolled onto my back and squinted my eyes together tight so just a few tears squirted from the corners as I carefully felt to see how much rock had lodged under my skin.

"Get up real slow," a voice said from up ahead of me. It startled me enough to make me forget the pain and, still lying on my back, I raised my head and could make out what at first seemed to be a tree among the many trees, but this one was slightly blurred, moving toward me.

"Who's there?" I called.

"Just get up, but slow," the voice said again, and by now I could make out a man's figure with what appeared to be a rifle held in one hand, sticking out from his side, pointing at the deep blue sky. "This is private property, I have to ask you to go back the way you came."

"I'm Mark Reilly, I live just up there." I managed to sit up and was slowly trying to stand without using my hands, which were also sore from the fall. "Are you related to the Hansons?"

He stayed about twenty yards away from me and I couldn't make out any of his features. I guessed he was Kate's husband, who was supposedly living out here with her for the month, but I couldn't figure out how to convince him to introduce himself.

"You're gonna have to go back. You can walk up along the field on the other side, if the Carrutherses don't mind."

"Please, we can work this out somehow. Would you like to come up to the house and have a beer with me? We can talk about this."

"Just go on." He let what appeared to be his rifle come down so the butt of it rested on the front of his shoe and leaned it out like a cane. I was standing now and my knees were starting to throb as the ripped skin bunched up. I could feel blood dripping down my shins. I decided I had no choice but to call him on it.

"Look, I just took a bad fall. My knees are bleeding. If you'd like to come up to the house to talk about this, that'd be fine. If not, I gotta get back." I fixed my vision on the blackness ahead of me where I knew the road forked and walked as quickly as possible past him and up the half-mile of my own driveway. I focused on the steady roar of the crickets as I made my way to the house. When I finally reached the house I looked over my shoulder and, seeing that he had not followed me, quickly went inside and locked the door behind me. I spent the rest of the night with the television on full volume, drinking a six-pack of beer and washing out my knees and elbows.

By the next morning I wondered if any of it had really happened. Get-Out-of-Here was scratching at the door and my head felt as sore from the beer as my joints did from the fall. By noon I knew I had to find out, so I got in the Civic and slowly crept down the driveway.

At the end of it, where it met the fork to the Hansons', there was a large post blocking my access to the shared road. On it was an ominous yellow sign informing me that trespassers would be prosecuted. I got out of the car and spent five minutes looking down the road and up the Hansons' part of the fork before wrestling the post out of the ground and lying it along the branches and weeds at the side. Then I jumped back into my car and drove as fast as pos-

> THERE WAS A LARGE POST BLOCKING MY ACCESS TO THE SHARED ROAD. ON IT WAS AN OMINOUS YELLOW SIGN INFORMING ME THAT TRESPASSERS WOULD BE PROSECUTED.

sible out to the county road, managing to avoid most of the potholes by memory.

I had lunch in Andree and spent a couple more hours going in and out of the few stores, where most of the merchants already knew my name, that I had been a high-school teacher in the city, and that I was working on a screenplay. I enjoyed talking to them more than usual, as it made me forget about what had gone on between me and the Hansons, and I nearly started to tell Renée, the cashier at the grocery store who was near my age and had taken a pointed interest in me, about the whole mess, but realized I only had two months on the hundred years the Hansons had been at Gooseberry Lake and I couldn't be sure where I really stood with anyone.

When I got back to the entrance of the shared road, I blinked. I drove past it and parked the car half in the brush along the county road so that branches pushed up against the passenger window. I then took my two plastic grocery bags and started walking alongside the edge of the field where I could see the Carrutherses' two-story farmhouse in the distance. I had never seen anyone out around that house and realized Lou at the post office had been right, they weren't getting around that much anymore. At the end of the field I turned into the woods, where I couldn't be sure whose property I was on but felt safe among the dense pine. The plastic bags were cutting into my hands and the bandages on my knees were starting to peel from the mile-long walk, but I finally made it to the house, dropped the groceries on the floor, and called Brenda.

    I knew he didn't have a father. I knew about everything there was to know about him. He'd stay nearly every day in my classroom for the hour after school until the late bus, happy to quietly read or study in the corner if I wasn't in the mood for talking. By the spring of his senior year I started driving him home myself, and he'd hang on my every word for the whole twenty-minute ride. He was my height and too thin. He had a long bowl of dark hair that he parted in the middle and kept hooked behind his big ears. His green eyes took up half his face, and I should know, because they were always looking at me. Everything about him seemed to stick out at an awkward angle, his ears, his shoulders, his feet, and even his hips. But in his eyes I had read every book, been to every city, seen every play, and known every type of person. Who wouldn't feel flattered?

    I was relieved when he left for Vassar in the fall, though he only lasted one semester. Reluctantly, I had agreed to see him a few times that summer before, a movie, coffee, and, finally, after he asked so many times, a camping trip to Lake Millacs. I felt I was providing the father figure his life had stolen from him. He was the best student I ever had, and when you're told how much you're responsible for that, you start getting more involved.

    "Don't get too involved," a friend of mine on the faculty had told me ten years before when

> BUT IN HIS EYES I HAD READ EVERY BOOK, BEEN TO EVERY CITY, SEEN EVERY PLAY, AND KNOWN EVERY TYPE OF PERSON. WHO WOULDN'T FEEL FLATTERED?

I first started the job. I doubt he would have said it if he hadn't known how inevitable it was at some point. The students became my life as I aged into my thirties and was no longer sure what exactly my life was made up of anymore.

I thought it would stop when he went away to college. I thought I could make it stop.

"I met your husband," I said to Kate, standing behind her at the post office.

She spun around, clutching letters and catalogs against her chest as if I was going to hurt her. Lou glanced out from his window, then busied himself with a package.

"I'm not happy about any of this," she whispered, and tilted her head slightly toward the door to indicate that we should talk outside, away from Lou. I followed her out. It had just rained and the air was heavy from it. We both instinctively looked up to gauge how long we could stand there talking.

"My husband is as upset as my mother, I'm afraid. They're a terrible combination." Kate looked better in the daylight; her skin had some color and her loose T-shirt made her seem more relaxed.

"Do you agree with them?" I leaned against the side of her Bronco, imagining it riding up and down the dirt road I hadn't seen in two weeks.

"I'm unhappy about the whole thing, but I know you have nothing to do with it."

"Tell them that."

"I've tried." A few drops of rain hit the puddles around us and one landed squarely on her forehead. She shrugged and glanced up, putting her hand on the Bronco's door handle right where I was leaning.

"What're July and August like?" I said, stepping away. She looked at me, confused. "Your sisters, June."

She gave me a forced smile and ducked into her Bronco right as the rain swept in.

June 1, 1998

Mark,

I'm sure you weren't expecting to hear from me so I'll be brief. Of course I was hurt when I called and found your phone disconnected and, when I called the school, to find out you had quit and left the city. Mrs. Anderson was very nice in the school office and passed along this P.O. Box number. I'm only sending this postcard because there aren't really any words to describe the hurt I'm feeling that you'd just leave like this and not tell me. What did I ever do to you? I would never hurt you like this.

Kelly

I always knew he'd find me again. Sometimes, after I had been down at the lake in the lawn chair that I would put in the water so I could sit and read with the lake up to my waist, I'd return to the house from the back, go in the kitchen doorway, and glance into the living room, where I expected to see him waiting for me on the couch. A few times I woke up in the middle of the night so sure that he was in the room with me that I'd have to switch a light on before remembering a dream I'd had with him in it. His laughter like a chicken, nervously filling in every breath I took when I told a story. His hands fluttering at me at any excuse to touch my sleeve, pull some piece of fuzz from my hair, palm me on the chest if I said anything *that* funny. The phone calls with no one at the other end. The headlights following too close. The branch snapping in the woods.

I heard the siren long before the knock on my door, so I had time to get out of bed, put the empty beer bottles under the sink, and pull on my jeans, shirt, and boots. When the policeman asked if I had seen any trespassers, I knew who he was talking about and asked him what he had found. He drove me to the end of my driveway to show me.

The headlights of a second police car and an ambulance made everyone look like owls. The men from the ambulance were over at the car, which was half off the Hansons' driveway, its front end embedded in a tree. The windshield was smashed and at first I could only stare at it until I followed voices and saw the man I presumed to be Kate's husband, though I had never really seen his face or heard his name. He was at the other police car talking to an officer who was writing everything down. I kept my gaze going up the Hansons' driveway until I saw Kate in what appeared to be an oversized white T-shirt and nothing else, her hands pulling down the edges of the shirt so it almost came to her knees. Before the policeman could say anything I walked over to the crashed car and the two ambulance men stepped away so I could see.

I must have told the officer he had been a student of mine. I remember him telling me he'd drive me back to my house and we could talk there. But just then I happened to look over at Kate and, as if I had given her a signal, she ran across the field of headlights to her husband and started beating him with her arms around the chest and head. In the glow of the lights she looked like a bird caught inside a house, wings desperately snapping against a barrier as invisible as glass. As he fell backward, his head hung down in protection from the blows, the police pulled her away. I then saw the rifle leaned up against the side of the police car where he had been standing.

"You're not charged with anything, there's just a lot of questions," Brenda told me the next day. We were sitting down by the lake, on my new lawn. "The bullet only grazed his shoulder. The impact of the crash snapped his neck. They think his foot floored the accelerator in reflex, from fear."

I had my head on my knees and stared out at the tree line on the opposite side of the lake. I wondered who lived over there. I had never seen a light.

I walked Brenda back to her BMW, which she had defiantly driven all the way up to my door. She held my hand and stopped when I did.

"You know what I keep thinking? That the last thing he thought was I fired that gun."

Brenda wiped at my face. It was over before it even started. Shock worked like that.

"Come on." She pulled me toward her car. "I'm driving you down to get that ridiculous blue thing you call your car."

I refer to it in my mind as the summer of no July and August, the summer June exploded in a fury and stayed all winter. The summer I got my very own road. Bill Hanson dealt directly with the Carrutherses, who sold him the strip of land along their field that connected to the woods of my own property. He put the whole thing in my name and also dealt with the men who took down the trees and cut out the road connecting me to the rest of Andree.

Roger Kerr (I finally learned his name from the newspaper) got two years for manslaughter in a plea bargain and I heard Kate filed for divorce. I never saw Ethel that summer and I probably wouldn't again, as she had taken to her bed and, according to Kate, seemed determined to stay there. Kate's sisters never came out that summer, at least not for their respective months of taking care of their mother. Kate elected herself to do it full time, though I only saw her a few times at a distance in town; I heard all this from Lou at the post office, who eagerly plied me with information without my asking, hoping I'd return a little, which I never did.

"Why do you stay?" Brenda usually managed to get in every phone call. "Your life doesn't have to be like Custer's last stand or something."

I could have answered that I stayed because somehow one gunshot made me feel like I had a hundred-year history in a town that had a lot of respect for family history. I could have said pride, but that didn't fit. Sometimes I felt that I stayed because on certain nights when I looked up at the stars over the lake it reminded me of the night I had spent with Kelly at Lake Millacs. How it had taken me hours to get the fire going and, once we were in our sleeping bags, it had immediately died out, and I heard a branch snap as he walked over to me, knelt down, put his hand on my cheek, told me he loved me. How from the forest floor the stars above us seemed reachable, distant lights on a shoreline I could swim to, and, after he cried, how much his body felt like a woman's.

Two Poems by David Lehman

February 28

God is the cloud that
travels with my caravan,
Bessie Smith is in my living room
singing "Do Your Duty," and
I may look like a gas station attendant
but my name is Jackson Pollock
and I'm the Big Bang Professor
of theoretical physics
at Southern Comfort University,
and as a good citizen
of this fading century
whose rules of sexual engagement
were laid down by the Marquis de Sade
I know I am responsible for all I see
which I have organized
into cities and chambers
as one might organize the sea

April 4

Fire engines in St. Mark's Place

Larry Rivers on saxophone

painting a man in formal evening clothes

spanking a beautiful Boucher bottom

with nylons and heels while I

photocopy the 1950s on your machine

the women eating soup at the counter

of B & H Dairy look even better

now that I've seen them nude on your walls,

dear Larry, who taught me how to see

French money and the Cedar Tavern menu

I must leave you now, yon water tower beckons

me to the roof where the sky retains its blue

as darkness descends in the empire of light

on Thirteenth Street and First Avenue

For the Bees
CELIA GILBERT

For Lois

We both remember the black and tawny carpet
of bees, moving over one another
in the glass box hanging in the schoolroom,
the waxen hexagons where they lived
the low roar of their endeavors.

Being close—awe—
with revulsion at their chaotic intimacy
that took no notice of us,
when freed from our orderly rows
we stared at their nakedness.

Like grownups, we could spy
on their secret places yet
could not fathom the steps of their dance
or how they turned their daily

flights into honey, when unconfined
they launched their awkward bodies
through the narrow exit to the sky,
tilling the fields, tracking the sun.

The teacher said they were workers
by which we understood, women,
since who but women would tend
larvae in their nursery?

Bees, we read,
transported the chariot of the Muses.
They stung the poets' lips
so they would create a bitter honey
from the meadows they roamed,
each poet with verses ready at her side:
hard retrieved distillation
of daily sunshot labors.

Under the classroom buzz we made
exchanging laughter and secrets,
helping the teacher clean the blackboard,
the furred mass vibrated.

FOR THE BEES

Before we ever dreamed

of wooden barracks,

piled logs with hollow eyes,

they enacted for us

the fearful community of the body.

Their mindful mindlessness

culled from the searchlight

of the sun the information

it desired

without knowing desire.

Encrypted, the bees rested and then,

unsepulchured, rose on the morning light,

while we moved to the sound of wings

that gave voice to an entity—

as the teacher taught us—

e pluribus unum,

out of many one,

we classmates of the boy

who hanged himself,

of a girl whose mother beat her,

we struggled and each day

brought home some residue of sweet

to store against our need.

SMOKE

CHIN HO CHONG

For William Matthews

I want to make this fade, the way a small,
blue pillar of smoke rises from the edge
of this cigarette, unfurling into a string

of curl in the stillness of the room. The smoke
thins and drifts in the lazy dance of a drunk
lost in the fog of his own senses. My first

year in America is a long blur of what
I don't remember except the kiss and
the face of that girl, her skinny legs

in white stockings, the blue denim dress
and black polished shoes she wasn't supposed
to play in but would. I didn't speak much

SMOKE

in first grade—my English was a rough music
of consonants and syllables—but I stole
a kiss from her anyway, wanting to let go

all the words I hadn't spoken. And if
my family hadn't moved, or if Maria and I
met again when we were old enough to have

learned about the tragedy of kisses, and if
I had the words to bring back something besides
the cheap sentiments of desire, the pennies

pitched against the schoolyard walls, and
the worthless triumph of remembering, I'd
let the slow burning embarrassment of that

moment be the lesson taught in the classroom
of a seedy bar, where a teacher and a student
sit at a table surrounded by ancient writings

of the drunk and lonely carved into the table,
recalling the names of all the women they once
wanted. Their faces appearing and disappearing

in the haze of smoke like an old film. We squint
for a better view.

A READABLE FEAST™

THE APPLE OF THEIR EYES

SARA PERRY

Sara Perry finds that Jane Austen, Alice B. Toklas, and Erskine Caldwell all baked a mean apple pie.

In the beginning, seeking perfection, Eve chose the apple. Smooth, round, fitting her palm, the apple's first luscious bite revealed a divine texture and heavenly taste. So ended Eve's and Adam's sojourn in paradise.

Despite the fact that the apple of the Garden of Eden was probably a peach or a pomegranate—translators misunderstood the Hebrew word *tappauch*—the apple's connection with the mythological contin-

ued, provoking wars and erotic encounters. Eventually a search for a different kind of perfection began, one that embraced the apple and created a culinary metamorphosis. Speaking more humbly, this was the search for the perfect apple pie, a pursuit shared by thousands of nameless souls, by myself, and by three extraordinary literary personalities whom I used as my guides.

I like the exotic. Apple pie needn't be

humbled by its down-to-earth nature and its simple ingredients. Alice B. Toklas, the apple of Gertrude Stein's provocative eye, proved this beyond doubt with a rich, single-crusted pie that was filled with a wine-infused puree, then embellished like a cake with a rum-butter icing.

"A rose is a rose is a rose," Gertrude would say (and Alice would embroider the line as small as a rose hip on handkerchiefs), but an apple pie in Alice's Parisian kitchen was certainly a departure from the expected.

In the decades between the First and Second World Wars, Stein and Toklas's avant-garde salon was a gathering place for painters, sculptors, and writers. Stein befriended many, including Matisse, Picasso, and Hemingway, providing them with good food, wit, and conversation. To the world, she was the writer and the genius and Toklas was her Cerberus, guarding her privacy while bouncing bores, creating feasts, and talking to the wives.

Toklas could read a recipe and a person with equal aplomb, judging the strengths and weaknesses of each. Hemingway didn't fare too well; she thought he was a braggart.

Alice B. Toklas. © Corbis

Erskine Caldwell. © McIntosh and Otis

techniques that made it special.

She was a remarkable woman in her own right. She had a sharp mind and a quick tongue. The author of two cookbooks, she had brusque opinions on the proper way to write a recipe. A New York editor, reviewing her second manuscript, queried the omission of serving amounts. She received a bristling response from Alice: "How should I know how many it serves? It depends—on their appetites—what else they have for dinner—whether they like it or not." (Did I mention she was quite sensible?)

As a young woman raised in San Francisco in the early 1900s, Toklas undoubtedly enjoyed the American standard, two-crusted, sliced-apple pie, but when she moved to France in her thirties, she came under the spell of continental cuisine and those

(In return, Hemingway never mentioned her name in *A Moveable Feast*, referring only to "Miss Stein and a companion.") In the kitchen, Toklas delighted in tasting a dish and unraveling the ingredients and

[continued on page 189]

THE APPLE OF THEIR EYES

• ALICE B. TOKLAS'S APPLE PIE •

Serves: Depends [says Alice]

INGREDIENTS:

2 1/2 pounds fresh cooking apples, quartered, cored, peeled, and cut into chunks (see sidebar)

1/2 cup granulated sugar

1/2 cup excellent red wine

1 9-inch pâte brisée (short-crust) pie shell, baked (see recipe on page 192)

1 1/2 cups powdered sugar

4 tablespoons unsalted butter

2 to 3 tablespoons good pale rum

Water for thinning

PLACE THE APPLES IN A LARGE, heavy pot. Cover and cook over low heat, stirring with a wooden spoon, until the apples are very tender, about 30 minutes.

Uncover the pot and stir in the sugar, wine, and butter. The apples will be soft and may still hold their shape. Turn the heat up to medium. Keep the mixture at a slow boil, stirring frequently until the apples cook down to a thick puree, 20 to 30 minutes. (To test the puree's thickness, run a spoon or a spatula along the pot's bottom. The puree should separate and remain apart for about 10 seconds.)

Remove the pot from the heat and let it cool. Run the puree through a food mill or processor until smooth and chill. The filling can be made up to 3 days ahead for maximum flavor. Makes about 1 1/2 cups.

To make the icing, stir together the powdered sugar, butter, and rum to a creamy, slightly runny consistency, adding a little water if necessary.

To assemble, pour and spread the chilled puree into the baked pie shell. Pour and lightly spread the icing over the filling. Let the icing set, about 20 minutes. Cut into small slices and serve.

JANE AUSTEN'S APPLE PIE

Serves 6

INGREDIENTS:

Short-crust pastry (see Toklas recipe on page 192)

2 pounds pie apples

1/2 cup water

4 tablespoons granulated sugar

1/2 crushed cinnamon stick

Grated zest of 1/2 small lemon

Softened butter as a garnish (optional)

PREPARE THE SHORT-CRUST in advance. Preheat the oven to 400 degrees.

Peel and core the apples. Place the peels and cores in a saucepan. Add the water and bring the mixture to a boil over medium heat. Reduce to low and continue to simmer until the liquid tastes like apples, about 20 minutes. Strain the liquid and return it to the saucepan. Add the cinnamon stick and 2 tablespoons of the sugar and slowly boil until the mixture is reduced to 1/4 cup, about 10 minutes.

Meanwhile, roll out the pastry dough according to the recipe. Cut a 1-inch strip along the outside edge of the rolled-out pastry circle. Grease the rim of a 9-inch pie plate and gently press the pastry strip over it. Slice half of the apples and place them in the pie plate. Sprinkle with 1 tablespoon of sugar and half of the lemon zest. Slice the remaining apples and place them on top of the first layer. Sprinkle the remaining 1 tablespoon of sugar and lemon zest over the apples.

Remove and discard the cinnamon stick from the reduced liquid and pour the liquid over the apples. Lightly moisten the top of the pastry strip with water and cover the filling with the reserved pastry circle. Trim off any excess. Press the crusts together with a fork and crimp to seal. Prick the top crust with the fork in several places. With a small sharp knife, cut several slits at right angles to each other between the center and edge of the crust and a small vent in the center

Place the pie on a baking sheet and bake until the crust is browned and the juices bubble up through the slits, 35 to 40 minutes. Cool on a wire rack for 3 to 6 hours before serving. This allows the juices to thicken and the apples to re-absorb some of the juice. If desired, when eaten warm, place a slice of butter on the top.

sublime French tarts. That's when she began to cook in earnest and her inventive mind went to work as she filled a buttery-rich pâte brisée (short crust) with slowly simmered apple-wine essence.

What reads like applesauce-in-a-crust turns out to be an elegant yet simple dessert. Cut into sweet slivers, it's a startling confection. From a woman who could be called plain, yet who dressed fashionably and wore remarkable hats, Toklas knew how to top off this culinary ensemble. She decked it with a potent, hard-sauce-style icing, making it the perfect pie for a Christmas or holiday feast. This is *not* a pie for a lost generation, and neither is her timely advice on cooking:

"Use only the best the market offers. If the budget is restricted, restrict the menu to what the budget affords. Cook with the very best butter, draw on your best wines. . . . This will exalt your effort, stimulate, intensify, indeed magnify the flavor."

The delectable perfume and enticing sweetness of an apple has always aroused our senses. Neolithic man found the glorious globe a scrumptious treat. Ancient Egyptians planted orchards to insure its constant supply, and by 200 B.C., the Romans were cultivating up to seven varieties. Today, there are two to three thousand varieties suitable for commercial growing, although supermarkets tend to carry only a dozen or so varieties that store

THE PERFECT APPLE PIE PRIMER

➤ *Apples are at their best in the fall and early winter.*

➤ *Choose the best, freshest blemish-free apples available. Look for locally grown varieties.*

➤ *Buy apples that are firm to the touch and use them within a few days.*

➤ *Keep apples refrigerated or in a very cool place. A centerpiece of apples spilling out of a bowl may look great, but an apple's flavor fades fast when stored at room temperature.*

➤ *To prepare several apples at one time, it's easiest to use a paring knife to cut each apple in quarters, then remove the core and the peel.*

➤ *Prevent peeled apples from turning brown by placing them in a bowl of lemon water. (1 quart water, juice of 1 lemon). Dry slices on a paper towel before using in a recipe.*

➤ *Cut apple wedges into 1/4-inch slices to hold their shape and texture while baking.*

➤ *4 small, 3 medium, or 2 large apples yields one pound of apples.*

➤ *One pound of apples yields 4 cups of sliced apples, 1 1/2 cups applesauce, or 3/4 cup puree.*

➤ *Apple pie in July? Sure, but not from local apples. Look in the market for apples from New Zealand, where winter is just beginning. Braeburns are a good choice.*

PIE APPLES

apples that hold their shape and texture

- *Braeburn*
- *Cox Orange Pippin*
- *Empire*
- *Granny Smith*
- *Jonathan*
- *Jonagold*
- *Northern Spy*
- *Rhode Island Greening*

SAUCE APPLES

apples that have a soft texture for smooth sauces

- *Cortland*
- *Empire*
- *Gravenstein*
- *Jonathan*
- *McIntosh*
- *Northern Spy*
- *Winesap*

well, stack well, and taste good. Regional farmers' markets and roadside stands are where the more unusual varieties can be bought and sampled.

Once you find a great-tasting apple, will it make the perfect pie? Not always. Some varieties, when cooked, lose their shape but are great for applesauce; others make terrific juice. Since it's not something you can tell by a look or a squeeze, ask the produce person for advice. Once you find the right pie apple and nestle it in a flaky crust, get ready to enjoy the quintessential comfort food and savory symbol of domestic bliss.

Some say apples and a pastry crust are like love and marriage. I think they're like love and sex: you can have one without the other, but it's better to have both. Erskine Caldwell, once one of the most widely read

twentieth-century American authors, had firsthand knowledge of sex and a very good idea of what makes a perfect apple pie.

In the 1940s, Caldwell was America's literary "big apple," selling more books than any other writer in American history. (By 1960, his books had sold more than sixty million copies.) He was one of the first writers to be mass-marketed in paperback—and to many of us of a certain age, he wrote our first flashlight-in-bed "dirty" book (*God's Little Acre* or *Tobacco Road*, take your pick). Caldwell's stories about the poor of the American South mixed social realism with sex and violence. Some thought his depiction of Dixie surpassed

Faulkner's. (Faulkner himself believed Caldwell to be one of America's five greatest novelists.)

Born in 1903 in Georgia, the son of a poor Presbyterian preacher who moved his son and wife from church to church, ministering to sharecroppers, Caldwell witnessed the desperate life of his characters and until the early 1930s struggled to make ends meet from his writing. In 1935, with the success of his play *Tobacco Road*, he became a celebrity. Soon after, he left his first wife, Helen, and their three children for Margaret Bourke-White, one of the country's most famous photographers. All of his relationships, including three more marriages, would be marred by jealously, betrayal, infidelity, and rage.

In 1938, a small red volume entitled *A Stag at Ease* appeared. Margaret Squire had embarked on the lofty aim of publishing "the culinary preferences of a number of distinguished male citizens of the world." With Carl Sandburg's cheese omelette, Jack Dempsey's macaroni and cheese, and A. A. Milne's crème brûlée, she was sure it would prove "a treasure trove for the hostess who aims to please."

Caldwell contributed a two-layer apple pie crust recipe, leaving the filling to be worked out by the reader. The kitchen is a revealing place, and Caldwell's omission is not so surprising from a man who saw the need to conceal and cover up. Whatever his motive, Caldwell's crust is a winner because instead of using butter for the fat and flavor, his recipe calls for shortening (for flakiness) and grated cheese (for flavor), which makes a lot of sense when you think about it. Cheese has always been a perfect partner

EATING APPLES

crisp, juicy apples for luscious eating

- ➤ *Braeburn*
- ➤ *Empire*
- ➤ *Fuji*
- ➤ *Gala*
- ➤ *Gravenstein*
- ➤ *Jonagold*
- ➤ *Mutsu*
- ➤ *Northern Spy*
- ➤ *Winesap*

• PÂTE BRISÉE •

MAKES 1 9-INCH PIE CRUST

INGREDIENTS:

1 cup all-purpose flour

1/2 cup (1 stick) cold, unsalted butter, cut into 8 pieces

Pinch of salt

About 3 tablespoons ice water, plus more if necessary

COMBINE FLOUR AND SALT in food processor; pulse once. Add the butter and pulse until the mixture resembles coarse crumbs, about 10 seconds. Some of the butter chunks should still be the size of small peas. (This can also be done by hand, in a bowl with a pastry cutter, two forks, or your fingertips.)

Place mixture in bowl and sprinkle with 3 tablespoons water. Stir with a wooden spoon or rubber spatula and gather the mixture into a ball. If too dry, add another 1/2 tablespoon water. When you can gather the mixture into a ball with hands, wrap it in plastic and flatten it into a small dish. Refrigerate for 30 minutes.

Sprinkle the counter with flour. Unwrap the dough and sprinkle with flour. (If the dough is too hard, let it rest for a few minutes until it gives a little when pressed with a finger.) For easy rolling, place the dough between two sheets of plastic wrap or inside a 2-gallon plastic freezer bag.

Roll from the center out. If dough seems sticky, dust with flour. Rotate dough and turn it over once or twice until the dough is about 10 inches in diameter and 1/8-inch thick.

Drape the dough over the rolling pin or fold into quarters. Place the dough into a 9-inch pie plate and press firmly into the bottom and sides. Trim the excess to about 1/2 inch all around, then tuck it under itself around the edge of the plate. Decorate the edge with fork or fingers. Refrigerate for 30 minutes.

Preheat the oven to 400 degrees. Line the pie plate with aluminum foil and fill it with dry beans. Bake for 15 minutes. Remove the beans and foil. Bake until the bottom of the shell is light golden, 10 to 15 minutes.

for apple pie. "Apple pie without cheese," say the English, "is like a kiss without a squeeze."

Time and time again, in the lean years, Caldwell left his family to write in solitude, and his letters reveal a diet that consisted of bread, cheese, and water. It's what he could afford; it's what tasted good and filled his belly; it was his comfort food. With the sweet taste of success—and the request for a recipe—Caldwell proved an intuitive cook. For those of us who like both sex and love (or pie crust and apples) I recommend combining Caldwell's crust with a fine pie apple, such as Jonagold, and a good sauce apple, such as McIntosh.

While there are countless recipes for apple pie, most are simply instructions. A favorite recipe—a perfect recipe—is like a culinary diary that reflects a delicious taste, a comfortable place, or a wonderful moment.

Before the late eighteenth and early nineteenth centuries, when professional cookbooks became available, most recipes were part of individual collections, handed down from one generation to the next, recording favorite dishes from decades back. English novelist Jane Austen, whose stories bring alive early-nineteenth-century middle-class life in England, depended on these recipes for her large and sociable family.

In Georgian times, dinner was often a lavish affair for friends and family. This mid- to late-afternoon meal might last for hours, with up to two dozen homemade dishes. Without today's refrigeration, providing the ingredients and cooking all this food was a consuming task. Staples such as fruits and vegetables were seasonal and usually homegrown.

The Austens had a family garden and a cellar or cold room, so that fruits such as apples and pears could be used year-round. While apples can be stored for months this way, the fragrant, delectable flavor quickly vanishes, as irrevocably as a golden autumn day. When making an apple pie, Jane and other cooks of her day wisely simmered the peels and cores to extract any nuance of flavor and used the liquid in the filling. They also relied on the tart and brilliant taste of lemon zest and the crush of spicy cinnamon to supply flavor when flavor was missing.

It may sound surprising, but in the fall and early winter, when I want to showcase apples at their peak, I go for Jane's pie every time. It's bottomless, so there's less crust to interfere with the taste of newly harvested apples. (I do cut back on the zest.) In the spring and summer months, when just-picked apples are only a memory but the longing for pie is immediate, her recipe is the one I crave. Then, the lemony perfume seems just right.

[continued on page 195]

ERSKINE CALDWELL'S APPLE PIE

SERVES 6 TO 8

· · · · · · · · · · ·

INGREDIENTS:

Pastry

2 cups all-purpose flour

1/2 teaspoon salt

1/2 teaspoon granulated sugar

1/2 teaspoon baking powder

3/4 cup cold shortening

1 cup cold grated sharp Cheddar cheese, such as Black Diamond or Vermont

4 tablespoons ice water, plus more if necessary

Filling

2 tablespoons unsalted butter

2 1/2 pounds (6 to 7) Jonagold apples, cut, cored, peeled, and quartered

1/2 pound (2) McIntosh apples, cut, cored, peeled, and quartered

1/2 cup granulated sugar

1/2 teaspoon ground cinnamon

Pinch of salt

1 teaspoon to 1 tablespoon lemon juice

· · · · · · · · · · ·

TO PREPARE THE PASTRY DOUGH, combine the flour, salt, sugar, and baking powder. Toss well to combine. Using a pastry blender, two knives, or your fingertips, cut the shortening into the mixture until it forms small clumps. (You can also do this in a food processor. See recipe on page 192.) Toss in the cheese. Stir evenly to combine.

Sprinkle in the ice water. Stir with a wooden spoon or rubber spatula and gather the mixture into a ball. If too dry, dribble in more water. When you can gather the mixture into a ball with hands, press it together to form a ball. Divide into two halves and wrap each half in plastic. Flatten each into small disks and refrigerate for at least 30 minutes.

To prepare the filling, heat the butter in a large skillet over medium-high heat. Add the apple slices, sugar, cinnamon, and salt. Once the apples begin to sizzle, turn the heat to low. Cover the pan and simmer the apples until the juices are released, about 8 minutes. The McIntoshes will begin to break down. Uncover and continue to cook over medium-high heat until the juices begin to thicken and the McIntoshes fall apart, about 5 minutes. Remove from heat and transfer the mixture to a bowl. Cool to room temperature. Add lemon juice to taste.

· ERSKINE CALDWELL'S APPLE PIE ·

[CONTINUED]

Preheat the oven to 400 degrees.

To roll out the crust, sprinkle a countertop with flour. Unwrap one portion of dough and sprinkle with flour. (If the dough is too hard, let it rest for a few minutes until it gives a little when pressed with a finger.) For easy rolling, place the dough between two sheets of plastic wrap or inside a 2-gallon plastic freezer bag.

Roll from the center out. If the dough seems sticky, dust with flour. Rotate and turn over once or twice until the dough is about 10 inches in diameter and 1/8 inch thick.

Drape the dough over the rolling pin. Place the dough into a 9-inch glass pie plate, pressing firmly into the bottom and sides. Trim the dough to 1/2 inch overhang. Add the cooled apple mixture, mounding and patting it slightly. Brush the edge of the bottom crust with water.

Roll out the remaining dough. Lay it over the apples. Trim the top and bottom edges to 1/2-inch overhang. Tuck so that the folded crust is flush with the lip. Press with fork tines to seal. Prick the top crust with the fork in several places. With a small sharp knife, cut several slits at right angles to each other between the center and edge of the crust and a small vent in the center.

Place the pie on a baking sheet and bake for 15 minutes. Lower the heat to 350 degrees until the crust is browned and the juices bubble up through the slits, about 35 minutes. (You may need to protect the crust edges with foil during the last 10 minutes.) Cool on a wire rack for 30 minutes to 1 hour. Serve warm.

Variation: For cheese lovers, grate an additional 1 cup sharp cheese and sprinkle it over the apple mixture before adding the top crust.

Each of my guides—Alice, Erskine, and Jane—showed me very different, yet perfect apple pies. I think, in the kitchen, perfection is a mingling of many different ingredients: imagination, hunger, history, and experience. Like the writer, I suppose, the cook takes off where nature left off.

The recipes have been tested by the author from primary sources. They have been rewritten for today's cook and, if necessary, ingredient amounts have been prudently revised for successful results.

THE LAST WORD

SICK ART

— or —

THE IMPORTANCE OF FEELING TERRIBLE

BENJAMIN ANASTAS

I. The first time I saw Damien Hirst's installation *Some Comfort Gained from the Acceptance of the Inherent Lies in Everything* (1996), I was suffering from a sinus infection, courtesy of my miserable office job. The details of my servitude are too grim to recount in any detail here, but I will say that my boss was a degenerate fraud with three identical briefcases, the ventilation was poor, and no matter how many times I cleaned my telephone with Windex it still smelled like one of my co-workers had been sucking on it. During idle moments, while my boss was raging at his subordinates behind a poorly soundproofed door, I imagined that work itself was a kind of rhinovirus, infecting my cells with a cruel efficiency and multiplying behind my eyes until I felt what can only be described as *rapture,* or, to quote Edmund Burke's *A Philosophic Enquiry into the Origin of Our Ideas of the Sublime and Beautiful* (1757), "a great and awful sensation of the mind." The symptoms of my pathetic sublime were postnasal

Caravaggio's Medusa © Corbis/Arte & Immagini

drainage, periods of nausea, facial pain exacerbated by straining or leaning forward, headache, malaise, and dizzy spells. I was in perfect shape, then, to visit Hirst's first solo exhibition at the Gagosian gallery in SoHo and gaze at his cow slices preserved in formaldehyde. Three years later the same piece would arrive at the Brooklyn Museum with the traveling *Sensation* exhibit and be denounced by Mayor Giuliani as "sick" and "disgusting." If only it were true! In my experience, feeling ill or suffering physical discomfort in the company of art can be a blessing and a privilege, and I defy the mayor, or any other seeker of consolation in a white-walled gallery, to convince me otherwise. Back to SoHo: On weekends the shoppers turn out in staggering numbers, and Gagosian was filled with members of the over-class that afternoon, taking in the show, as they do everything, with the pretense of ownership, as if a snap of the fingers or the flash of a credit card will buy them everything in sight. I saw no blemishes, no matter how I longed for an imperfect face, and heard no sniffles (save my own). A woman posed beside the cow installation while her friend snapped a series of pictures. A crowd gathered around Hirst's giant ashtray and peered inside at hundreds of cigarette butts scattered at the bottom and faintly reeking. Shopping bags scraped against my legs as I walked around the gallery, taking in the strange collusion between the artist and his audience and feeling sick to death with the artlessness of it all, so I ducked into the space between two particularly gruesome cow slices and felt the earth move, unsure, in the end, if this tremor was a result of my sinus infection or of the neatly packaged spectacle around me: the anatomy of an animal laid bare for a passing thrill, a "delightful horror" in the words of Edmund Burke, returning the viewer's thoughts, as all art should, to mortality and the fragile beauty of what comes before: life.

2.

Hunger increases the appetite for art, as I learned during a pauper's vacation in Venice. My girlfriend and I had been offered an apartment in Santa Croce for the month of July, when the natives flee the seasonal invasion of tourists, and we arrived with heavy luggage, high expectations, and very little money between the two of us. I was waiting—and waiting, and waiting—for a wire payment from the publisher of my first novel, and immediately began wasting ten-thousand-lire phone cards on calls to the Chase Manhattan service line, hoping, each time I dialed, to discover a dramatic change in my account balance. There are certain pay phones in

Venice that I remember just as vividly as Giorgione's *Tempest* (c. 1500), and there were fruit and vegetable stalls at the Rialto Market—colorful and fragrant still lifes—that I approached with more reverence, even, than Bellini's stunning altarpiece from the San Zaccaria church, *Madonna and Child Enthroned with Saints Peter, Catherine, Lucy, and Jerome* (1505), which we didn't see so much as experience in the luminous hours before dinner. We survived on fruit, sandwiches, and pasta (strictly rationed) and on nightly trips to a cheap *gelateria* just behind the Frari church. All told, I was a clueless traveler in this, the only city that I know of where reality and artifice are indistinct. When I think of Venice, now, I remember footsteps, and Istrian stone facades, and a storm the day before the Redentore festival that littered the Fondamenta Zattere with the colored remains of paper lanterns and flooded the pavement between Spirito Santo and the salt warehouses past our ankles. Our apartment was above a failing souvenir shop on the Campo Santa Maria Mater Domini (even now I love intoning the name), and the owner, who let her son run wild in the square, would break that city's blessed silence with screams of *Michele!*, followed by a tirade of abuse that led my girlfriend, a native Italian speaker, to mutter about Italian parenting and close the window shutters. Most days ended with the family downstairs in full meltdown—Michele whimpering, mother raging, father storming off—and after a while it seemed that vacationing child abusers, having caught wind of Michele's plight, began showing up below our windows after dark to deliver swift and voluble punishments. Hunger pangs, thunderstorms, silence, a spanking, the lapping of water against stone, the ringing of countless church bells . . . and a clear-etched vision that came from having just enough to eat and not one calorie more, rendering us speechless on a wooden bench beneath Tintoretto's *The Fall of Manna* (1592–94) in the sunlit and cav-

> *All told, I was a clueless traveler in this, the only city that I know of where reality and artifice are indistinct.*

> *I nearly staggered into Peter. I'm having a stroke, I thought while the painting swam before me; I stepped back from the banquet table just as a museum guard rose reluctantly from his chair to warn me off.*

ernous San Giorgio Maggiore. Of this painting and its complement, *The Last Supper* (also 1592–94), Henry James wrote:

> You get from Tintoretto's work the impression that he felt, pictorially, the great, beautiful, terrible spectacle of human life very much as Shakespeare felt it poetically — with a heart that never ceased to beat a passionate accompaniment to every stroke of his brush.

By this time the wire deposit had finally posted on my bank account, too late, in the way of all things monetary, to quiet our sense that we were lacking. Somehow three weeks had run out on us—we were due to leave Venice in twenty-four hours, and were trying, on that final day, to fit in just a few more churches, a drink at Harry's Bar, and dinner out—gasp!—at a restaurant. No last supper (real or imagined) would sate me more, though, than the one reproduced by Veronese in his *Feast in the House of Levi* (1573), a teeming banquet set underneath the shelter of a Renaissance arcade with Christ at its central axis, the disciples nearby, and Turks, animals, dwarves, drunks, and German soldiers crowding in from outside the picture frame, evidence of life beyond the confines of scripture. The painting hangs by itself on a wall of the Academia now, and on the night when we visited the museum, early in our stay, my girlfriend had oversalted our minestrone so severely that I nearly staggered into Peter. I'm having a stroke, I thought while the painting swam before me; I stepped back from the banquet table just as a museum guard rose reluctantly from his chair to warn me off. What happened next is a mystery, but when my girlfriend wandered back a few minutes later I was sitting on a bench and staring openly at Christ. "Are you all right?" she asked, and what could I say? Maybe it was just the sodium, or the city's romantic atmosphere, or the distance we had traveled to reach that particular room, because I was feeling terrible, and the painting looked sublime.

3.

For some time now I've been aware of the art world's dirty little secret: looking at the stuff, actually standing there and looking, is an unpleasant experience, sometimes even agonizing. The visual arts can, on occasion, provide what Longinus in his treatise *On the Sublime* defined as *ekstasis,* or transport, but for most of us, the first instinct upon entering a bright-white gallery is to swivel on our heels and flee. I don't know exactly why this is, and believe me, I've been over and over the subject in my mind, bluffing my way, in the process, through some of the world's most important art museums. How I suffered through them all! Sure, the collection at the Uffizi includes Piero del la Francesca's *The Duke and Duchess of Urbino* (c. 1472), but a Florentine jazz musician and his girlfriend cut me in the admissions line, and my hours there were lost in a rage so fierce that only Caravaggio's glaring *Medusa* (1590) could soothe me. Sleeplessness, dehydration, and a child riding his Italo—Big Wheel over cobblestones ruined a visit to the Capodimonte Museum in Naples, and in London—giddy London—a sneaking suspicion that I was really back in Cambridge, Massachusetts, marred the Tate and the National Gallery—not to mention the school group that nearly pushed me face first into the Rosetta Stone while I was enjoying a peaceful moment at the British Museum. In an effort to regain my composure I went down into the basement and found myself, after taking a wrong turn or two, in a bare, musty-smelling room filled with fragments of Roman statuary: a marble morgue displaying heads, torsos, arms, and legs of widely different scales (all stolen, of course) and so close to human that my stomach turned. Here a delicate bare foot, there a head topped with spiral curls, and, resting on a pedestal, a broken Nike missing both her wings . . . And in the corner a man with unwashed hair and a greasy parka stood before an easel drawing body parts in charcoal, which stained his hands, shadowed by an expressionless museum guard. What kind of sick fuck, I thought, enjoys this?

Only an artist.

Acrostic

John M. Daniel

To solve: Fill in the words from the clues provided and transfer the letters to the corresponding squares in the grid. When complete, the grid will reveal a quotation. The author and the source of the quotation will be spelled out by the first letters of the words defined. Solution on page 209.

CLUES

A. Pram, infested..

B. American furrier, born in Waldorf, Germany in 1763..
C. Angling equipment (3 wds.)..........................
D. 1944 song by Harold Arlen (4 wds.)...........

E. "From where the sun now stands, ____ no more…" (3 wds., Chief Joseph, 1877)......
F. Mertz or Merman..
G. Generous..
H. The last word of "Ulysses"........................
I. "My ____", film starring Daniel Day Lewis (2 wds.)..
J. "I am ____ so simple," lyric borrowed by Cole Porter from Word Q (4 wds.)...........

K. Morning moisture.......................................
L. "____ Got to be Taught," song from "South Pacific," 1948................................
M. Wanderers..
N. Unwell..
O. 1930 song by Willard Robison (3 wds., after "A")...

P. "It is as difficult to appropriate the thoughts of _____ it is to invent." (2 wds., Emerson, "Quotation & Originality")......
Q. Shakespeare play that inspired "Kiss Me Kate" (4 wds., after "The")......................

R. "___ dollar for every…" (5 wds.)..............
S. Where Judy Garland's boyfriend lived in "Meet Me In St. Louis" (2 wds.)................
T. "To___, to forgive divine" (3 wds., Alexander Pope, "Essay on Criticism")............

WORDS

__ __ __ __ __
128 22 86 93 73

__ __ __ __ __
159 109 20 44 96
__ __ __ __ __ __ __ __ __
53 88 72 36 92 14 168 51 108 26
__ __ __ __ __ __ __ __ __
161 145 35 75 59 78 120 13 19 95
__ __ __ __
142 137 84 134

__ __ __ __ __ __ __ __ __
111 131 32 70 82 43 170 18 144 63
__ __ __ __
54 143 114 129 16
__ __ __ __ __ __ __ __
10 156 174 81 149 117 28 39 58 116
__ __ __
104 150 12

__ __ __ __ __ __ __
23 15 166 130 100 47 124 175

__ __ __ __ __ __ __ __ __
110 146 94 55 118 141 38 42 64 3
__ __ __ __ __ __ __
87 74 173 8 153 106 61 160 127
__ __ __ __ __ __ __
147 133 102 40 33 25 7 79

__ __ __ __
9 155 119 4 98
__ __ __ __ __
46 125 158 30 139 56
__ __ __
1 90 99

__ __ __ __ __ __ __ __
122 11 49 113 65 2 69 21 167 152
__ __ __ __
31 101 83 132

__ __ __ __ __ __ __
76 136 176 148 37 24 103 126

__ __ __ __ __ __ __ __
66 27 107 135 138 164 105 89 121 60
__ __ __ __
34 177 140 52 5 80
__ __ __ __ __ __ __ __ __
162 77 17 169 68 91 123 71 154 115

__ __ __ __ __ __ __
85 165 171 67 112 48 57 45

__ __ __ __ __ __ __ __
29 157 151 41 97 50 6 172 163 62

1 N		2 O	3 J	4 L	5 Q		6 T	7 K		8 J	9 L
	10 G	11 O	12 H	13 D		14 C	15 I	16 F	17 R	18 E	19 D
20 B	21 O	22 A	23 I		24 P	25 K	26 C	27 Q	28 G	29 T	
30 M	31 O		32 E		33 K	34 Q	35 D	36 C	37 P	38 J	39 G
40 K		41 T	42 J		43 E	44 B	45 S		46 M	47 I	
48 S	49 O	50 T	51 C	52 Q		53 C	54 F	55 J	56 M	57 S	58 G
	59 D	60 Q	61 J	62 T		63 E	64 J	65 O	66 Q		67 S
68 R	69 O		70 E	71 R	72 C	73 A		74 J	75 D	76 P	
77 R	78 D	79 K		80 Q	81 G	82 E	83 O	84 D	85 S	86 A	
87 J	88 C		89 Q	90 N	91 R	92 C	93 A		94 J	95 D	96 B
97 T	98 L	99 N	100 I		101 O	102 K	103 P	104 H		105 Q	106 J
	107 Q	108 C		109 B	110 J	111 E	112 S		113 O	114 F	115 R
116 G		117 G		118 J	119 L	120 D	121 Q		122 O	123 R	124 I
125 M	126 P	127 J		128 A	129 F	130 I	131 E	132 O	133 K	134 D	
135 Q	136 P		137 D	138 Q	139 M		140 Q	141 J	142 D		143 F
144 E	145 D	146 J		147 K	148 P	149 G	150 H	151 T	152 O	153 J	154 R
	155 L	156 G	157 T		158 M	159 B	160 J	161 D	162 R	163 T	164 Q
165 S		166 I	167 O	168 C		169 R	170 E	171 S		172 T	173 J
174 G	175 I	176 P	177 Q								

[203]

Contributors

YEHUDA AMICHAI was born in Germany in 1924 and emigrated with his family to Israel in 1936. He has published eleven volumes of poetry in Hebrew, two novels, and a book of short stories. His work has been translated into thirty-three languages. His collections of poetry available in English include *The Selected Poetry of Yehuda Amichai: Newly Revised and Expanded Edition* (1996); *Yehuda Amichai: A Life of Poetry, 1948-1994*; *Even a Fist Was Once an Open Palm with Fingers* (1989); *Poems of Jerusalem* (1988); *Great Tranquillity: Questions and Answers* (1983); *Love Poems* (1981); *Time* (1979); *Amen* (1977); *Songs of Jerusalem and Myself* (1973); and *Poems* (1969). He lives in Jerusalem.

BENJAMIN ANASTAS is the author of *An Underachiever's Diary* (1998) and is currently completing his second novel, *The Faithful Narrative of a Pastor's Disappearance*. He lives in New York City.

FRANK BURES is a writer living in Portland, Oregon. He has lived in Italy and Tanzania, and is currently at work on a book, *Mt. Meru's Edge: Essays from Tanzania*, selections of which have appeared in *Salon* and *Outpost* magazines.

PHOTO BY JON DUDER

NICHOLAS CHRISTOPHER is the author of seven books of poems, including *The Creation of the Night Sky* and the forthcoming *Atomic Fields: Two Poems*. He has also published three novels, including *Veronica* and the just-published *A Trip to the Stars*, and a nonfiction book, *Somewhere in the Night: Film Noir and the American City*. He is currently at work on a new novel, *Franklin Flyer*. He lives in New York City.

JAMES CONRAD's first novel, *Making Love to the Minor Poets of Chicago*, will be published by St. Martin's Press/Thomas Dunne Books in March 2000. He is also a graphic designer and lives in Manhattan and Woodstock, New York. Originally from Minnesota,

PHOTO BY KEVIN KEITH

CONTRIBUTORS

he received his B.S. from Northwestern University and his M.F.A. from Columbia University. His poetry has appeared in *The James White Review, Fruit,* and the *Allegheny Review.* "Road" is his first published short story.

CHIN HO CHONG is a graduate of the University of Oregon's Creative Writing Program and has attended the Bread Loaf Writers' Conference and the University of Maryland's M.F.A. Program. One of the founding members of the Poison Clan Collective, he resides in Los Angeles. *Smoke* is his first published poem.

JOHN M. DANIEL is the author of *Play Melancholy Baby*, a mystery novel; *The Woman by the Bridge*, a story collection; *The Love Story of Sushi and Sashimi*, a cat book; *One for the Books*, a memoir; and *Structure, Style & Truth: Elements of the Short Story*, a writing-instruction book. He lives in Santa Barbara, California, where he runs a literary small press and is on the faculty of the Santa Barbara Writer's Conference.

CELIA GILBERT's most recent book is *An Ark of Sorts,* which won the first Jane Kenyon Chapbook Award. Her two previous books of poetry are *Bonfire* and *Queen of Darkness*. Her work has appeared in *The New Yorker, Poetry, Grand Street,* and *Ploughshares,* among other places. She is the winner of a Discovery Award, a Pushcart Prize, and awards from the Poetry Society of America. She lives in Cambridge, Massachusetts, where she is also a printmaker.

PHOTO BY DEBI MILLIGAN

PHOTO BY CHRISTOPHER BIERLEIN

NEIL GORDON is the director of electronic publishing at *The New York Review of Books* and *Granta,* editor of the New Fiction Forum at *The Boston Review,* and author of two novels, *Sacrifice of Isaac* and *The Gun Runner's Daughter*. He holds a Ph.D. in French literature from Yale University, and his articles and reviews have appeared in the *New York Times Book Review, The Village Voice,* and the *San Francisco Chronicle*. He lives in Brooklyn, New York.

AMY HEMPEL is the author of the story collections *Tumble Home, Reasons to Live,* and *At the Gates of the Animal Kingdom*. She has edited, with Jim Shepard, *Unleashed: Poems by Writers' Dogs* (1995).

PHOTO BY KENNETH CHEN

ROBERT H. HETHMON was born in Paducah, Kentucky, in 1925. He was educated at Tennessee-Knoxville, Cornell, London, and Stanford. He was a teacher of theater for

CONTRIBUTORS

forty years at Colorado, Wisconsin-Madison, California-Riverside, and UCLA. At Wisconsin he founded and directed the Wisconsin Center for Theatre Research. He is the author of *Strasberg at the Actors Studio.* Hethmon has three sons and five grandchildren. During a long life he has also been a stagehand, soda jerk, soldier, rabbi's assistant, and self-rising man in a flour mill. His main avocation is mountaineering.

GERALD HOWARD is executive editor of Doubleday Broadway.

MARK KLETT is represented by the Fraenkel Gallery in San Francisco and the Pace Wildenstein/MacGill Gallery in New York. His work is currently on display at the Etherton Gallery in Tucson. He lives in Tempe, Arizona.

DAVID LEHMAN's most recent book is *The Last Avant-Garde. The Daily Mirror*, which includes "February 28" and "April 4," has just been published by Scribner. In 1988, Lehman launched *The Best American Poetry,* of which he is now the series editor. He is the author of three collections of poems: *An Alternative to Speech* (1986), *Operation Memory* (1990), and *Valentine Place* (1996). He has also written four critical books including *The Line Forms Here* (1992) and *The Big Question* (1995). He is the general editor of the Michigan Press Poets on Poetry Series, and teaches at Bennington, Columbia, and the New School for Social Research.

J. ROBERT LENNON is most recently the author of the novel *The Funnies* (1999). His first novel, *The Light of Falling Stars* (1997), won the Barnes and Noble Discover Great New Writers Award for 1997. His short fiction has appeared in *The New Yorker, Harper's, Story, Fiction,* and *American Short Fiction.* He lives with his wife and son in Ithaca, New York.

EDDIE LITTLE is the author of the novel *Another Day in Paradise.* He won the Association of Alternative Newsweeklies award for best columnist. He is working on an original screenplay for Paramount, and his second novel, *Steel Toes,* will soon be published by Viking Penguin. He lives in Encino, California.

MIAN MIAN was born in 1970 in Shanghai, China, where she presently lives. She is a rock-and-roll deejay and a rave-party organizer, as well as the author of the story collection *La La La* and the novel *Candy,* both written in Chinese.

CONTRIBUTORS

JOHN FREDERICK MOORE is a New York–based writer who frequently covers literary topics. His work has appeared in *Salon* and *Poets & Writers*.

JONATHAN NAPACK first wrote for *Spy* magazine in 1991 before taking on the *New York Observer*'s contemporary-art column for five years. During that time, he also wrote features for such magazines as *GQ*, *Vogue*, and *New York*. Since 1997, he has been based in Hong Kong, where he covers avant-garde and pop culture from Tokyo to Jakarta for the *International Herald Tribune* and various magazines. He is currently writing a book about art, subculture, and revolution in Asia.

ED OCHESTER has two books of poetry forthcoming: *Cooking in Key West*, a chapbook; and *The Land of Cockaigne*. His most recently published books are *Allegheny* (Adastra) and *Changing the Name to Ochester*. He is the editor of the Pitt Poetry Series and (with Judith Vollmer) of the magazine *5 AM*.

TIM PAGE is the artistic advisor and creative chair of the St. Louis Symphony Orchestra. Until recently, he was the chief music critic for the *Washington Post*, where he won the Pulitzer Prize for criticism in 1997. He began his research into the life and work of Dawn Powell in 1991, working closely with the author's family to win release of her papers. Since then, he has edited collections of her best novels, her diaries, her letters, her plays, and her short stories and has written the first biography of her.

SARA PERRY is a columnist for *The Oregonian*, a food and restaurant commentator for KINK-FM radio, and a contributor to food and travel publications and Web sites. She is the author of ten cookbooks, including *The Complete Coffee Book*, *The Chocolate Book*, and *The Complete Book of Herbal Teas*; and her most recent, *Christmastime Treats* (Chronicle Books), is part of her holiday celebration series, with recipes and crafts for the whole family. She lives in Portland, where some of the tastiest pie apples grow.

PHOTO BY JOANNA E. MORRISSEY

MARGE PIERCY is the author of fifteen collections of poetry including *What Are Big Girls Made Of?* and *The Art of Blessing the Day*, a collection on Jewish themes. Leapfrog Press recently brought out a collection of her early and uncollected poetry, *Early Grrrl*. She has published fifteen novels, all of which are in

PHOTO BY IRA WOOD

CONTRIBUTORS

print, including *The Longings of Women; Storm Tide*, written in collaboration with her husband, Ira Wood; and, most recently, *Three Women*.

PHOTO BY JERRY BAUER

ROBERT POLITO received the National Book Critics Circle Award for *Savage Art: A Biography of Jim Thompson*. His other books include *Doubles* and *A Reader's Guide to James Merrill's The Changing Light at Sandover*. He directs the graduate writing program at the New School for Social Research in New York City.

PATTIANN ROGERS has published nine books of poetry. *Firekeeper: New and Selected Poems* was named one of the best books of 1994 by *Publishers Weekly*. *The Dream of the Marsh Wren* and *Writing as Reciprocal Creation* appeared in 1999. *Collected and New Poems: 1981–2001* is forthcoming from Milkweed Editions. Other titles include *A Covenant of Seasons,* a collaboration with the artist Joellyn Duesberry. Ms. Rogers has been the recipient of two NEA grants, a Guggenheim Fellowship, and a poetry fellowship from the Lannan Foundation. In 1997, she was awarded *Poetry*'s Frederick Bock prize, and this year she won her fifth Pushcart Prize.

JOHN SANFORD was born Julian Shapiro in 1904. He published his first stories in *Contact*, and his first novel, *The Waterwheel*, in 1934. Of his numerous books, his most recent appeared from the University of Illinois as part of their Radical Novel Reconsidered series. His upcoming book, *A Palace of Silver*, is a celebration of his wife, who died ten years ago. This spring, Sanford was awarded a lifetime-achievement award by the *Los Angeles Times*. He lives in Santa Barbara, California.

CHARLES SIMIC's first full-length collection of poems, *What the Grass Says,* was published in 1967. Since then, he has published more than sixty books in the U.S. and abroad, including *Jackstraws* (1999); *Walking the Black Cat,* which was a finalist for the National Book Award in poetry; *A Wedding in Hell; Hotel Insomnia; The World Doesn't End: Prose Poems,* for which he received a Pulitzer Prize for poetry; *Selected Poems: 1963-83;* and *Unending Blues*. He also has published many translations of French, Serbian, Croatian, Macedonian, and Slovenian poetry and four books of essays, most recently *Orphan Factory*. His many awards include fellowships from the Guggenheim Foundation, the MacArthur Foundation, and the National Endowment for the Arts. He is a professor of English at the University of New Hampshire.

CONTRIBUTORS

PHOTO BY MICHEL DELSOL

LYNNE TILLMAN's fiction includes the novels *Haunted Houses, Motion Sickness, Cast in Doubt,* and *No Lease on Life* (finalist for the National Book Critics Circle Award in fiction, 1998), as well as two collections, *Absence Makes the Heart* and *The Madame Realism Complex.* Her nonfiction includes *The Velvet Years: Warhol's Factory 1965–1967* and *The Broad Picture,* an essay collection. *Bookstore: The Life and Times of Jeannette Watson and Books & Co.* was recently published by Harcourt Brace.

SALLIE TISDALE is a contributing editor at *Harper's*. Her sixth book, *The Best Thing I Ever Tasted: The Secret of Food,* has just been published by Riverhead. Currently a Pope Foundation Fellow for a work about retarded adults, she lives in Portland, Oregon.

PHOTO BY MARK BARNES

LISA ZEIDNER is the author of four novels, most recently *Layover,* and two books of poems. Her stories, articles, and reviews have appeared in *GQ,* the *New York Times,* and elsewhere. She is director of the graduate program in English at Rutgers University.

PHOTO BY KEN YANOVIAK

ACROSTIC PUZZLE SOLUTION
(puzzle on page 202)

J.M. Barrie
My Lady Nicotine

"I gave up my most delightful solace, as I regarded it, for no other reason than that the lady who was willing to fling herself away on me said that I must choose between it and her. This deferred our marriage for six months."

. . . .

A. Buggy
B. Astor
C. Rod and reel
D. Right as the Rain
E. I will fight
F. Ethel
G. Munificent
H. Yes
I. Left Foot
J. Ashamed that women are
K. Dewdrops
L. You've
M. Nomads
N. Ill
O. Cottage for Sale
P. Others as
Q. Taming of the Shrew
R. I wish I had a
S. Next door
T. Err is human

Note:
J.M. Barrie (1860-1937) is best known as the creator of Peter Pan, the boy who wouldn't grow up. In the late 1880s, he wrote a series of newspaper stories about a group of London bachelors, young bohemian chaps who had nothing in common except their devotion to a particular smoking mixture. These stories were gathered together in 1890 and published as a book, My Lady Nicotine, which is considered the finest literary tribute to pipe-smoking. It is even more a hilarious satire of late Victorian society, and it is also a fine celebration of bachelorhood. Like Peter Pan, the nameless narrator and his goofy friends (who could have taught Bertie Wooster a thing or two) have no intention whatsoever of ever growing up.

PACIFIC NORTHWEST COLLEGE OF ART: CONTINUING EDUCATION

PNCA Continuing Education courses fit even the most difficult of schedules. Classes are available in both the fine and graphic arts fields including computer courses & BFA foundation courses. Adult programs are offered in the evening and academic credit is optional. Weekends feature an extensive young adult and children's program.

To request a catalog or for more information: call 503-821-8895
1241 NW Johnson, Portland, OR 97209
Spring Semester: February 7-May 7

Or register on line at www.pnca.edu

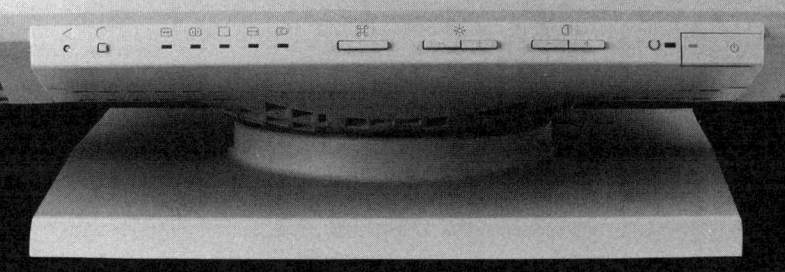

Discover the Writer's Life in New York City

Master of Fine Arts in Creative Writing

Over more than six decades of steady innovation, The New School has sustained a vital center for creative writing, with a faculty that has included some of this century's most acclaimed poets and novelists. The tradition continues with our MFA in Creative Writing, offering concentrations in **fiction, poetry, nonfiction** and **writing for children.** Study writing and literature with The New School's renowned faculty of writers, critics, editors and publishing professionals.

Faculty 1998-1999: Hilton Als, Jill Ciment, Jonathan Dee, Cornelius Eady, David Gates, Lucy Grealy, Amy Hempel, A.M. Homes, David Lehman, Pablo Medina, Rick Moody, Francine Prose, Luc Sante, Dani Shapiro, Jason Shinder, Darcey Steinke, Abigail Thomas, David Trinidad, Susan Wheeler, Stephen Wright.

Visiting Faculty: Ai, Martin Asher, Frank Bidart, James Ellroy, Margaret Gabel, Glen Hartley, Pearl London, Thomas Mallon, Carol Muske, Geoffrey O'Brien, Robert Pinsky, Jon Scieszka, Ira Silverberg.

Director: Robert Polito

Fellowships and financial aid available.

For a catalog and application contact:
212-229-5630 ext. 251
or email: admissions@dialnsa.edu

New School University
The New School
66 West 12th Street New York NY 10011

New books at half price! And you're not shopping at the Strand?

Not just *some* new books, tens of thousands of them. We have reviewers' copies, promotional copies of current books from all over the country. At half the new-book price.

Want more? How about the largest selection of Used, Rare, and Art books in the world? 50% off on paperbacks. Fine leather bindings for as little as $15. It's the kind of shopping you can do only at the Strand.

✶ Free Catalogs ✶

828 Broadway (at 12th St.)
Mon-Sat: 9:30AM-10:30PM Sundays: 11:00AM-10:30PM
(212) 473-1452   Fax (212) 473-2591   Email: strand@strandbooks.com

STRAND BOOK ANNEX
95 Fulton St. (3 blocks east of Bway) Mon-Fri: 9:30AM-9:00PM Sat-Sun: 11:00AM-8:00PM

JOHNSON: If you take black people out of the last two hundred years of American history, you don't have American history.

NAYLOR: You have nothing. You have no music. You have no nothing.

JOHNSON: It wouldn't exist. And American democracy wouldn't exist either. That to me is the telling point.

NAYLOR: You know what else would not exist? White people would not exist, if you took black people out of the equation. Because their identity depends on not being what you are.

> "We need writers to look at difficult issues in a sophisticated manner. Rikki Ducornet has done this. She is a mirror of our innermost selves and she gives us back to ourselves." — *The Nation*

The Monstrous and the Marvelous

With the great Renaissance voyages to the New World came the popularity of *Wunderkammern*, or cabinets of wonders, in which newly discovered monsters and marvels could be displayed. Like such a cabinet, this collection of essays surveys the monstrous and the marvelous—as transmuted in the alembic of Rikki Ducornet's open-hearted vision—in literature, art, and film. For her, excess, anomaly, and heterodoxy entice the imagining mind to embrace "otherness," enlarge the world, and regenerate Eden.

0-87286-354-9 $12.95

Entering Fire

A startling and brilliantly comic novel that scrutinizes the sources of fascist mentality in nations and, potentially, in all humans.

"*Entering Fire* displays a cheerfully gruesome audacity and an imagination both lively and bizarre." — *The New York Times*

"*Entering Fire* takes on some of the biggest issues of the 20th century....For sheer power, inventiveness and verbal density, [it] is the best read I've come across for a long time." — *The Observer*

0-87286-355-7 $10.95

CITY LIGHTS BOOKS can be purchased at your local bookstore or ordered directly from City Lights Mail Order
261 Columbus Avenue, San Francisco, CA 94133.
Ph: (415) 362-8193 Fax: (415) 362-4921 or via our website:
www.citylights.com